It's important to take stock of your ⟨...⟩ n. Are you living out your God-given purpose? ⟨...⟩ holding you back? Do you need to hit a reset ⟨...⟩ our life? *Free to Lean* will help you answer the⟨...⟩ You'll experience new freedom as you read th⟨...⟩

ARLENE PELLICANE
Speaker and author of *31 Days to Becoming*

Insightful and genuine, *Free to Lean* extinguishes the lies we've come to believe about our identity in the world while rekindling a passion for who we were created to be in Christ. Grab a friend and a highlighter and be prepared to say goodbye to "mom guilt" forever!

APRIL LAKATA CAO
Military wife, mom of four, writer, coffee drinker, yarn hoarder

This book spoke to my "lopsided" (and rather exhausted) soul. How often I've struggled to please people—or even myself—over seeking to please my Lord. *Free to Lean* reads like a friend sharing advice over a cup of tea. I can't wait to share this book with friends. The discussions it will spark are sure to encourage and challenge me in an even deeper way.

AMY LANSER
Recovering people-pleaser, wife, mom, recent transplant to a Midwestern state

Finally! Someone put words to my scrambled thoughts and guilty feelings about balance. Ladies, do yourselves a huge favor. Read this book. Let God's truth shared through Jocelyn saturate your being, and His Spirit help you put these principles into practice.

CARRIE DAWS
Author, blogger, and almost empty nester

Jocelyn's unfiltered snapshots of her experiences and the personal reflections of other women offer biblical encouragement to fully lean in to God's direction for your life, no matter the season. *Free to Lean* provided the kind of exhaling freedom and direction my heart needed.

MINDY WISSINK
Wife, homeschool mom, craft hobbies enthusiast

Free to Lean gave me permission to do as God says. I love Jocelyn Green's clear writing style carefully crafted with Scripture references. The book is an encouragement to this busy career woman and mother. I am refreshed to know that as I pursue God's life for me, His opinion is the only one that matters.

JAIME JO WRIGHT
Author and Professional Coffee Drinker

Free to Lean encourages women in all seasons in life to find empowerment beyond the world's expectations. With warmth, humor, and a reminder of the stability found in Jesus, Jocelyn Green challenges us to take a breath. Sit, reflect, accept that your topsy-turvy life is in someone's control. Don't worry. He's got this.

RACHEL MCMILLAN
Author of the Herringford and Watts series, frequent scribbler, bookworm, and Torontonian

Free to Lean empowers women to let go of their fear, insecurity, and inadequacies and live in the freedom, assurance, and grace of who God created us to be. As a military wife and mom of three teenagers, I love how this book offers me a reprieve from the unnecessary pressure of being it all and doing it all.

NATALIE WALTERS
Writer, blogger, and avid tea drinker

Free to Lean illuminated the darkened corners of my spirit with godly truth and wisdom, allowing me to reflect on my life's path with greater joy and contentment. It brought me tremendous encouragement. I felt as though the book had been written especially for me during this particular crossroads of my life as I and my family are experiencing changes in our ministries and careers.

ELLEN AYERS
Wife, mom to two boys, home economist, administrative assistant

Free to Lean is definitely the book all women need to read. Jocelyn gives us great advice on making peace with our lopsided lives. If you are ready to be free, then *Free to Lean* is for you.

CRYSTAL SCOTT
Devoted follower of Christ, homeschool mom, blogger

Do you always bite off more than you can chew? This book gives women clarity to focus on the important things in life and let go of the rest. I plan on sharing this with other women who have a lot on their plate and rereading myself when I need reminding of when to say NO! and when to ask for help.

KAREN HEERKES
Mom, wife, and hairstylist/therapist

This book was exactly what I needed. I recommend it to every woman out there. Are you feeling insignificant, like you're not doing enough, or are you constantly comparing yourself and your gifts to others? If you answered yes to either question, you have to read this book. I was so encouraged and motivated to really lean on God.

JEANETTE DURKIN
Follower of Christ, wife, mother, and teacher

Free to Lean is the secret handbook to navigating life's bumps in the road. It was just what I needed to hear (on so many levels)—and I will want to hear again! Perfect to reread in every season in life, this book is a keeper!

DONNA PURKEY
Navy wife, mother of two, teacher, author, sustained by God's great grace

God has used *Free to Lean* to refresh my spirit. Reading *Free to Lean* is like sitting around a table at a coffee shop with your mentors, gleaning wisdom from their life experiences. Through Scripture, personal experience, and the experiences of others, Jocelyn Green gives tangible examples of struggles and biblical helps for leaning into Christ and finding the freedom that purposely living for Him offers.

KERRY THATCHER
Mother of five and recovering bookaholic
(at least until a new Jocelyn Green book is published)

free to lean

MAKING PEACE WITH YOUR LOPSIDED LIFE

JOCELYN GREEN

Discovery House.
from Our Daily Bread Ministries

Free to Lean: Making Peace with Your Lopsided Life

© 2017 by Jocelyn Green

All rights reserved.

Discovery House is affiliated with Our Daily Bread Ministries, Grand Rapids, Michigan.

Requests for permission to quote from this book should be directed to: Permissions Department, Discovery House, P.O. Box 3566, Grand Rapids, MI 49501, or contact us by email at permissionsdept@dhp.org.

Any undocumented stories and quotes from individuals in this book are from private interviews conducted by the author. In each case, the persons and events portrayed have been used with permission. To protect the privacy of these individuals, some of the names and identifying details have been changed.

Interior design by Rob Williams, InsideOutCreativeArts.com

ISBN: 978-1-62707-678-4

Printed in the United States of America
First printing in 2017

TO THE ADVENTURE CLUB

Contents

FOREWORD

I love something Oswald Chambers once said: "Let God be as original with other people as He is with you."

God knows how to manage the entire universe, but He simultaneously leads each one of us in the way that *we* should go. At this very moment, He's drawing one of His children up close, under His wing for protection, while at the same time He's sending another out onto the battlefield. God trains, heals, reveals, corrects, redirects, restores, and promotes us, all at different times, all in different seasons, because we're all in very different places on our journey. He's a personal God who delights in every detail of our lives (Psalm 37:23). There's no one-size-fits-all when it comes to God's dealings with His children.

This is important because we humans have an uncanny ability of taking what God is revealing to us and making rules for other people. For some reason, we just love to judge each other, pressuring people to fit into a box that we believe defines the mature, balanced, successful Christian life.

Yet we're *all* works in progress. And Jesus's victory on the cross sets us free to be a work in progress, without condemnation. Isn't that good news?

God—the One who put the stars in their places—knows exactly what *you* need right now. His instructions for you are perfect, and they'll revive your soul (Psalm 19:7). As you *lean in* and listen to that still, small voice, He will strengthen your frame, heal your soul, bring clarity to your thoughts, and provide fresh power to your purpose. He does that uniquely for you, while simultaneously doing the same for me. Awesome, yes?

Still, life has its twists and turns. The landscape changes and the elements rage, sometimes without a moment's notice. What may be obedience for us in one season will take us out of God's will in the next. So how are we supposed to navigate the fluctuating terrain of our lives?

Read Jocelyn's title again—*Free to Lean*—and you'll find the answer there. If we focus more on status than we do stewardship, we'll lose our way. If we emphasize results more than we do faithfulness, we'll burn ourselves out. We are free to lean, invited to lean, and promised that if we do lean into Jesus, great things will come. Fruit. Life. Rest. Restoration. Abundance.

The leaning life reminds us that we can do *nothing* outside of our intimate connection to Jesus. And it's in this place of leaning, depending, abiding, and trusting in Jesus that we learn we don't have to be all things to all people—we just need to stay in step and in rhythm with the Lord.

If your shoulders ache from carrying too heavy a load, or if you're just plain tired of trying to be all things to all people, you've come to the right place. This book is an invitation to a deeper, more settled life. *Free to Lean* is jam-packed with wisdom and insight that's biblical and wonderful. Keep reading, and you'll see what I mean.

May God himself meet you personally and profoundly as you embrace your current life season. Jesus invites you to rest in Him, be much with Him, and to accomplish great things because of Him. You can trust Him in this season, and the next.

Susie Larson
Talk radio host, national speaker,
and author of *Your Sacred Yes*

INTRODUCTION

Then Jesus said to his disciples, "Whoever wants to be my disciple must deny themselves and take up their cross and follow me. For whoever wants to save their life will lose it, but whoever loses their life for me will find it."

MATTHEW 16:24–25

Jesus never said, "If any want to become my followers, let them deny themselves, take up their cross and lead a balanced life." He said to follow him. He wants us to do what he would do if he were in our place.

JOHN ORTBERG
The Life You've Always Wanted

Put all your trust in Him!

My palms were sweating. On the other side of a massive desk, my high school guidance counselor scrutinized me with narrowed eyes until I felt like a head of lettuce at the grocery store. He was evaluating my chances of being awarded college scholarships, and had just reviewed my activities:

Make a choice – Follow Him – not my way

Honors choir and vocal ensemble.

Theater.

Yearbook staff.

Piano teacher.

disciple – student of Jesus

National Honor Society.
Top of my class academically.
President of service club.
Vice president of my class.
Secretary for student council.
Board member for the city's Teen Trust nonprofit.

My counselor cringed. "Could you play volleyball?"

"Um, I don't think so," I stammered. It wasn't that I didn't see the value of sports and teamwork and healthy competition. I'm just, aside from my piano-playing fingers, woefully uncoordinated.

"What about golf? Basketball? Could you be a cheerleader, at least?"

I gaped at him. "I'm not at all athletic, and besides, I don't have time." I tapped the list on his desk by way of explanation.

"Yes . . ." He tapped my list of commitments himself. "Music. Academics. Leadership. You're not very well-rounded, are you? If you really want to be competitive for scholarships, we should really balance out your high school career with at least one sport. You know, so that you can be the complete package."

My heart sank. I was not enough, not complete, he was telling me, because I wasn't balanced.

NOT BALANCED

I'm still not balanced. But I am focused. I concentrate more than I juggle. My life's portfolio is not broadly diversified, which shouldn't be a big deal since I'm no longer competing for college scholarships. I'm married, have two kids, two pets, and a writing career. I'm doing what I love, and what I feel called to do. And I still hear voices telling me to pursue balance as a goal in and of itself.

I bet you hear them, too. But I love the way John Ortberg, author of *The Life You've Always Wanted*, describes what he calls "the paradigm of balance." The idea "simply doesn't capture the sense of compelling urgency worthy of human devotion," he says. "It lacks the notion that my life is to be given to something bigger than myself."[1]

And yet, the common refrain among time-starved, noise-saturated, overworked Americans is, "How can I achieve balance?"

We've been asking the wrong question. Nowhere in the Bible does God tell us to pursue balance. If you're a believer, your purpose in life is far bigger than that. Jesus said that being His disciple requires us to deny ourselves, to lose our own lives so we can find life in Him (Matthew 16:24–25). As we follow Jesus, with our crosses on our backs, we aren't balanced—we're leaning, hard, after our Savior, whatever that may look like in our own particular seasons of life.

If we define *balance* as a state of equal attention to equal priorities, a static, even-keeled division of time, Jesus himself was not "balanced." In their book *God in the Marketplace*, Henry and Richard Blackaby remind us that Jesus once spent forty days in fasting and communion with His Father. Sometimes He escaped the crowds around Him by going to the mountains alone to pray through the night. Jesus occasionally shared meals with His disciples, but would also forego eating to accomplish other things. One time, asleep on a boat, He was so weary that even a dangerous storm didn't wake Him. "Jesus lived his life with passion but not necessarily with balance," the authors say. "Yet at the close of his life, he concluded, 'I have glorified You on earth by completing the work You gave Me to do' (John 17:4). Likewise, at his death, Jesus triumphantly cried: 'It is finished!' (John 19:30). What was his secret? He constantly sought his Father's agenda, and his Father consistently showed him what he should do that day (John 5:19–20, 30)."[2]

Thanks for the work prepared especially for me.

A TIME FOR EVERYTHING

Friends, balance is not the goal. We are free to lean in whatever direction God is calling us. A lopsided life is not a disordered life: flowers tilt toward the light and the oceans gravitate toward the moon. Why, then, should we not lean into our season of life?

I love the alternative framework for a well-lived life developed by pastor and author Bruce B. Miller. Balance, he writes, burdens us with "guilt over not giving adequate attention to every priority every time," while rhythm offers "peace in releasing expectations that do not fit this time in life and in setting a healthy pace for activities."[3] Rhythm allows us to move and adjust with the seasons, and according to an ancient sage famous for his God-given wisdom, there are plenty of those:

> There is a time for everything,
> and a season for every activity under the heavens:
> a time to be born and a time to die,
> a time to plant and a time to uproot,
> a time to kill and a time to heal,

a time to tear down and a time to build,
a time to weep and a time to laugh,
a time to mourn and a time to dance,
a time to scatter stones and a time to gather them,
a time to embrace and a time to refrain from embracing,
a time to search and a time to give up,
a time to keep and a time to throw away,
a time to tear and a time to mend,
a time to be silent and a time to speak,
a time to love and a time to hate,
a time for war and a time for peace.

ECCLESIASTES 3:1–8

Whether it's a time to build or tear down, to run or rest, to raise small children or start a company, we have the freedom to order our days accordingly, without guilt. I don't know about you, but this alone breathes peace into my spirit already. We get to lean into the current season, understanding that other seasons will follow.

LEANING IS THE WAY FORWARD

When it comes to sailing, leaning often accompanies movement and progress. I'll borrow from my husband's experience to illustrate.

Between Rob's third and fourth years at the United States Coast Guard Academy, he was required to sail from New York City to Copenhagen, Denmark, on the USCGC *Eagle*, a three-masted barque. To maneuver the tall ship, the crew must handle twenty-two thousand square feet of sail and five miles of rigging. When the sails catch the wind, the ship lists, or leans, either toward port or starboard, up to a grade of 30 percent. The hands on deck compensate by shifting their weight as they move about. The crew members who are off duty must strap themselves into their racks (beds) to keep from tumbling to the floor. It's possible to move forward without listing, but rare. Leaning from side to side doesn't indicate trouble—it's just how the vessel must respond to the wind and waves.

Just as the *Eagle* lists so it can move toward its destination, I lean into my calling to achieve what God wants me to do. It takes some practice to keep my feet steady beneath me. Sometimes I stumble and wipe out on deck. But that doesn't mean I should take down the sails just so I can stand calmly. It only means I need more practice.

Still, the sailing ship doesn't always list so steeply—sometimes the sailors lessen the degree so it's more comfortable for the crew to take their meals. Sometimes the ship is skimming the waves at seventeen knots and other times it's moving less quickly. After reaching port, she rests. There's a rhythm to how a ship sails across an ocean, and the *Eagle*'s methods must change depending on the situation. Jesus's methods varied, too—He feasted and fasted, slept through a storm and pulled an all-nighter. And we must follow that example as well.

WHAT TO EXPECT FROM THIS BOOK

This book is an honest conversation, an exploration of the heart issues behind a life that leans, and of the biblical pillars that will support us and keep us from falling over. This book is for you if:

- you've tried balance and are ready for something more
- you feel burdened by the expectations placed on your life by others—even yourself
- you find yourself in a time of specific demands, whether by your choosing or not, and want to learn how to navigate it

In the first five chapters, we'll discuss what it means to live on purpose. We'll shed false guilt for not spending our energy where God never called us to invest. We'll expose the myth of measuring up to impossible standards, examine the voices that crowd our heads, and explore what it means to seize God even when we're too exhausted to seize the day. In the second half of the book, we'll look at five pillars that support a life that leans: consistent connection, elastic boundaries, breathing room, prayerful vision, and amazing grace. Along the way, you'll meet others who are leaning toward their God-given purpose, and some whose lives seem lopsided due to circumstances not of their choosing.

Free to Lean relies heavily on biblical insights. I pray that you already have a personal relationship with Jesus Christ. If you don't, or if you're unsure, please see the section called "Knowing Jesus Personally" at the back of the book.

WHAT THIS BOOK IS NOT

This book is not a platform for me to suggest all women should lead the same life. Life is not one-size-fits-all, and only you and God can determine the best course for you and your family. *Free to Lean* is not about forcing you into any manufactured expectations—it's about you finding freedom and peace in doing what God has called you to do.

This book is also not a how-to guide on cramming more into your life. *Free to Lean* is less about self-help and more about God-help as you strive to align yourself with His purposes for you right now, today. I hope it will help you find wholeness, peace, and freedom.

HOW TO USE THIS BOOK

Free to Lean is appropriate for individual reading, but it will be even more effective if you have a friend or small group of women reading along with you. Questions for personal reflection are provided, which can also guide you in your group conversations if you choose. Swap your own stories and discuss whatever is on your heart at the end of each chapter. You may want to reserve some of the answers for your own journal if they're too personal to share, but I'd encourage you not to let that stop you from talking to a trusted friend or two about what you're processing. You'll be invaluable sounding boards for each other as you sort out what the Lord is revealing to you.

Every once in a while, that old conversation with my guidance counselor rattles around in my head. *Not very well-rounded. Need to balance you out so you can be the complete package.* If you have ever felt pressured to "do it all"—whether you work outside the home or in it, whether you're single or married, whether you're fresh out of college or retired—this book is for you. We're all leaning, sometimes so far we're in danger of falling over. But are we complete? Absolutely. We are already complete in Christ, no matter what (Colossians 2:10).

Now, are you ready to make peace with your lopsided life? Let's get started!

God's
Riches
At
Christ's
Expense

PART ONE

The Leaning Lifestyle

CHAPTER 1

Life on Purpose

The LORD will fulfill his purpose for me;
your steadfast love, O LORD, endures forever.
Do not forsake the work of your hands.

PSALM 138:8 ESV

He gives us a purpose in life, not because He needs us,
but because He loves us.

SUSIE LARSON

Your Beautiful Purpose: Discovering and Enjoying
What God Can Do through You

I was in heaven even before the plane touched down. Adrenaline burst through my jetlag. Below our Boeing 737, veiled in pearl grey mist, were Big Ben, Parliament, Buckingham Palace, the Tower Bridge, and the River Thames. London was my new home—at least for a month.

January of my freshman year in college was spent studying British literature and poetry in England, with London as our home base. My fellow classmates and I toured Shakespeare's Stratford-upon-Avon; visited the London home of John Keats; ate in C. S. Lewis's favorite Oxford pub; and read the original manuscript of *Beowulf* and poems by Elizabeth Barrett Browning in the British Museum. You'd think that those experiences would have seared a dozen sonnets in my mind, right?

Well, that was twenty years ago. And while that month further endeared literature, history, and travel to me, I only remember two poems with clarity: John Donne's "A Valediction: Forbidding Mourning" because I wrote a paper on it, and T. S. Eliot's "The Love Song of J. Alfred Prufrock" because of one haunting line: "I have measured out my life with coffee spoons."

Honestly, it makes me shudder. Perhaps timid, indecisive Prufrock meant simply that his life's accomplishments amounted to nothing more than that which could be measured by spoons. But I've always leaned toward a literal interpretation, if only because it scares me even more, this idea that an entire life could be lived with nothing to show for it but the passing of time—which he marked by the count of coffees consumed. This type of meaningless life, to me, is more frightening by far than any gothic horror penned by Edgar Allan Poe. I can't help but take quick stock of my life: At the end of it, will it be measured out in dishes washed? In books read or written? In church services attended? In bills paid, weeds pulled, socks matched and tucked safely back into drawers? Surely, surely, there is more to life than mere tally.

Christ died so we might live abundantly. He did not die so we could count our lives away, but so that our lives would count for eternity. We are made in the image of God. We matter. To believe otherwise is to despair.

To pursue wholehearted living, we need a firm grasp on our purpose. And I assure you, it goes well beyond coffee spoons. So what on earth are we here for?

THE DECLINE OF FEMALE HAPPINESS

A study conducted by the National Bureau of Economic Research found a concerning trend: despite clear gains in gender equality since the 1970s, women are growing un-happier. Over a thirty-year period, researchers found that women have been measurably less happy than men. Why?

One section of the study offers clues. Women were asked to rate how important each of the following areas were to them:

- Being successful in my line of work
- Having a good marriage and family life
- Having lots of money
- Having plenty of time for recreation and hobbies
- Having strong friendships
- Being able to find steady work
- Making a contribution to society
- Being a leader in my community

- Being able to give my children better opportunities than I had
- Living close to parents and relatives
- Getting away from this area of the country
- Working to correct social and economic inequalities
- Discovering new ways to experience things
- Finding purpose and meaning in my life

The responses were striking. Young women are attaching increasing importance to thirteen of the fourteen domains, with the only exception being "finding purpose and meaning in my life." Researchers Betsey Stevenson and Justin Wolfers explain, "These data arguably suggest that women's life satisfaction may have become more complicated as the women have increased the number of domains in which they wish to succeed."[1]

Naturally, if we want to succeed in thirteen areas of life, chances are we won't meet our own standard in at least some of them. What I find illuminating—and sad—is the lack of importance placed on finding purpose and meaning. Living life without purpose is like navigating without a compass. It's just . . . wandering. Purpose tells us how to prioritize our time. Purpose tells us how to fulfill the time, not just fill it. Purpose gives satisfaction and makes sacrifices worthwhile.

MAN'S SEARCH FOR MEANING

The question of purpose affects more than our happiness and unhappiness. As Jewish psychiatrist Viktor Frankl discovered while imprisoned at Auschwitz, meaning can be the difference between life and death. When a prisoner lost faith in meaning and in his future, "he also lost his spiritual hold; he let himself decline and became subject to mental and physical decay."[2]

Frankl later developed what he named logotherapy for his patients, founded on the idea that the pursuit of life's meaning is motivating for all humankind. He wrote:

> There is nothing in the world, I venture to say, that would so effectively help one to survive even the worst conditions as the knowledge that there is a meaning in one's life. . . . In the Nazi concentration camps, one could have witnessed that those who knew that there was a task waiting for them to fulfill were most apt to survive. . . .
>
> What man actually needs is not a tensionless state but rather the striving and struggling for a worthwhile goal, a freely chosen task. What he needs is not the discharge of tension at any cost but the call of a potential meaning waiting to be fulfilled by him.[3]

As a believer, I find Frankl's Auschwitz observations and his theory of meaning to be fascinating. There is a healthy tension pulling us from who we are to who we are to become. Purpose is healthier for us than a tensionless, or stress-less, state of being. The fact that God "has also set eternity in the human heart" (Ecclesiastes 3:11) bears witness to the fact that mankind craves meaning.

MEANINGLESS?

The meaning of life is an age-old question that King Solomon tackled in the book of Ecclesiastes. Throughout its twelve chapters, as Solomon examines wisdom, pleasure, work, and wealth, the word *meaningless* appears about thirty-five times. The key phrase "under the sun" is used twenty-seven times in the New International Version, representing what this present world has to offer. The distinction is an important one, meaning that our own pursuit of happiness will fall short unless it relates to God and His kingdom. "A person can do nothing better than to eat and drink and find satisfaction in their own toil. This too, I see, is from the hand of God, for without him, who can eat or find enjoyment?" (2:24–25). The New American Standard Bible puts verse 24 this way: "There is nothing better for a man than to eat and drink and tell himself that his labor is good."

The Bible has a lot to say about work. One of my favorite verses is Ephesians 2:10: "For we are God's handiwork, created in Christ Jesus to do good works, which God prepared in advance for us to do." Not only did God create us, but He prepared good works for us to do. These tasks are specific to us, and He has equipped us to do them.

Take a close look at this: "So God created mankind in his own image, in the image of God he created them; male and female he created them. God blessed them and said to them, 'Be fruitful and increase in number; fill the earth and subdue it. Rule over the fish in the sea and the birds in the sky and over every living creature that moves on the ground'" (Genesis 1:27–28). Notice that these verses come before Adam and Eve sinned in the Fall. In the paradise that was the Garden of Eden, right after mankind was created,

God *blessed* them and gave them work to do. When we work—whether as paid employees, artists, volunteer staff, or as parents to our children—we bear the image of our Creator God. Bearing His image brings Him glory.

Psalm 8 echoes the theme. From this passage, we understand that God cares deeply for us and that He made us to rule over the works of His hands. The work He delegates to us allows us to bear His image and, ultimately, bring glory and majesty to His name.

Bearing God's image and bringing Him glory, my friends, is the ultimate purpose for the Christian life. Time and again in the Scriptures, we see this truth laid out for us:

> *"For the sake of his great name the LORD will not reject his people, because the LORD was pleased to make you his own."*
> 1 SAMUEL 12:22

> *"In the same way, let your light shine before others, that they may see your good deeds and glorify your Father in heaven."*
> MATTHEW 5:16

> *"Neither this man nor his parents sinned," said Jesus, "but this [blindness] happened so that the works of God might be displayed in him."*
> JOHN 9:3

So, if purpose is our life's compass, and God's glory is our true north, how do we get there? What does that look like for women today?

BIG-PICTURE PURPOSE

For each one of us, God has overarching purpose for our lives, purpose that involves using our unique set of gifts and abilities in the sphere of influence He has assigned us. Whether you work in the home, business, medicine, science, nonprofits, education, sports, ministry, service occupations, or the arts, stewarding your particular gifts with excellence brings God glory. When we see this purpose clearly in our lives, we are blessed indeed.

What about those who find themselves in a place that is not their area of expertise or passion? Though we may not be able to see God's purposes in certain seasons of life, He still uses us in these spheres to bring glory to himself. God doesn't waste the valleys in our lives. We must trust His promise not to forsake us (Matthew 28:20) and remember that His ways are not our ways (Isaiah 55:8).

When I worked as an editor for a nonprofit in Washington, DC, I was confident that my work had purpose. At the Council for Christian Colleges & Universities, I was using my skills in ways that honored God, and I could see the difference our work made.

Then I married a Coast Guard officer, and we moved to his next duty station of Homer, Alaska. I went from living and working in the nation's capital to being unemployed in a town of four thousand people. I wasn't even Jocelyn anymore, but "the XO's wife." (Rob was the XO, executive officer, of his ship.) I was fully committed to being a supportive wife, but with Rob gone seven months out of the first year of our marriage, even that was a challenge. Through no fault of my husband, it seemed to me that when I packed up my apartment and moved forty-five hundred miles northwest, I'd left both my purpose and my identity behind.

PURPOSE IS NOT IDENTITY

Before we move on, let's be clear about this foundational truth: our purpose is not the same thing as our identity. Your current role is not the sum of who you are.

"When I was a stay-at-home mother, I thought not working outside the home made me a 'good' mom," writes author and counselor Brenda Yoder. "When God called me to work in public schools, it contradicted what I thought a Christian mom should do. My identity was shaken. When I asked God to show me what it meant to be a godly woman, He told me it was being obedient to Him, no matter where I was. That was the first time I realized my identity was not based on my parenting role or profession, but on my position as His daughter."[4]

The way God works out His purposes in and through us may change over time, and there may be seasons when we don't see any purpose in what we're doing. But who we are never changes, and cannot be taken from us. *We are not what we do.* Our purpose is important, but not more important than who we are in Christ. If you find yourself unsure of your purpose—or if you know what it is but feel like life has derailed you from it—repeat after me:

> *I am not what I do. I am not less for what I don't do. I am created in the image of eternal God (Genesis 1:27), complete in Christ (Colossians 2:10), fearfully and*

*wonderfully made (Psalm 139:14). I am a child of God
(1 John 3:1). I am a co-heir with Christ (Romans 8:17).*

When we confidently claim our identity in Christ, we won't be threatened by a change in roles. Let's define who we are by *whose* we are, not by what we do.

Thirteen years after my time of unemployment and discouragement in Alaska, I can see how God used the experience to work out His purposes for my good and His glory. He used that time to grow my faith and passion so I would later be able to encourage other military wives through my first book, *Faith Deployed*, and the books that followed. God certainly had a clear purpose for my husband when He moved us to Alaska. But I wasn't just "tagging along"—God had a purpose for my life with that move, too.

Married or single, older or younger, whatever our background, each one of us gets our very own purpose. Carolyn Custis James writes:

> God has a unique plan for each woman. We are called not to sit on the sidelines but to be players, active contributors, to run the race He has marked out for us. If God is sovereign, then every day of our lives has meaning and purpose because God has planned it. We are not left in the wake of God's plan for someone else. No matter how intertwined our lives become with the lives of husbands, friends, and family members, God's plan for us is individual and personal.[5]

For those of you who long for a life of significance but feel so trapped in the minutiae of daily life that you can't imagine how it can be part of God's plan, let me gently remind you that you are not forgotten. Wherever you are, God sees you, and He hears you. The work He began in you, He'll be faithful to bring to completion (Philippians 1:6).

For many of us, motherhood is the thing that demands the most stretching and changing of ourselves. When I first met my friend Lisa at a professional conference, I could tell right away that she was talented, organized, and intentional about pursuing her career. I predicted she'd meet whatever goals she set for herself by the time I saw her at the following year's gathering. Yet her sense of purpose has been challenged and her goals changed by the responsibility of motherhood. "There are so many things that I want to do that I feel like I've had to put aside during this season," she told me. "I've spent countless hours in prayer, telling God that none of this 'life stuff' was making sense, that I was supposed to be pursuing my professional passions in a way that felt more productive and efficient *alongside* raising my little ones . . . but God seems to have a different path for me."

Lisa admitted that her God-directed path has "far less professional production" than she'd hoped, but "far more inner soul growth and healing while He teaches me what it means to be a servant, a wife, and a mother." While her own upbringing in a Christian home had been less than ideal in many respects, "God has been reshaping my foundation as a daughter in Christ, and has gently whispered that 'the time will come' for the other passions and interests."

THE DAILY CALL

Whether we're living out our big-picture purpose or we're in a season of waiting and trusting, we are always expected to represent Christ. This is our daily call. No matter what our agenda holds, we can reflect His image when we love our neighbors, model Christlikeness in our interactions with others, and bear the fruit of the Spirit (Galatians 5:22–23). This is a calling and a purpose that always applies.

My friend Kathleen, who loves her full-time ministry position as director of outreach, missions, and spiritual development for her church, learned the reality of the daily call over a tough period of six years when she worked in an unfulfilling job filled with tension. She had moved to the area to care for her mother, who was fighting cancer—and that offered more meaning than Kathleen could have imagined.

Twice, she lived with her mother for three months at a time. For two years, Kathleen accompanied her mom to most of her doctor appointments, chemotherapy infusions, and radiation treatments. "I heard her talk of heaven and saw the excitement in her eyes when she imagined living there with Jesus, and with my dad, who had died years earlier," she told me. "I heard the wisdom she'd gained in studying the Bible over the years and hearing what new things God was teaching her, even in the midst of her dying. My empathy and grace has grown through both my parent's deaths, but particularly by walking with my mom in her journey to heaven—and I'm exceedingly grateful for that."

Perhaps you too are in a season that seems, at first glance, a departure from what you perceive your life's overarching purpose to be. Or perhaps you're blessed to be in the most fulfilling role you've had yet, just as Kathleen is now. Either way, our daily call is the same: to bear the image of Christ to those around us.

In his letter to the Ephesians, Paul wrote, "Therefore I, the prisoner of the Lord, implore you to walk in a manner worthy of the calling with which you have been called, with all humility and gentleness, with patience, showing tolerance for one another in love, being diligent to preserve the unity of the Spirit in the bond of peace" (4:1–3 NASB). This is a universal charge. Whatever we do during the day, whoever we reach in our spheres of influence, we are to "be imitators of God, as beloved children; and walk in love, just as Christ also loved you and gave Himself up for us, an offering and a sacrifice to God as a fragrant aroma" (5:1–2 NASB).

The word *walk*, which we read in the verses above, emphasizes the constancy of the charge. We are not called to be imitators of God when we feel like it, or just on Sundays or holidays, or even when we are most likely to be noticed and rewarded for "good deeds." Instead, we are to "walk . . . worthy" and "walk in love" with every step we take. It doesn't get more daily than that.

When it comes to life purpose, human nature is to think that bigger is better. The more visible the work, the more people reached, the more successful and meaningful it must be. But God's economy doesn't work that way. We are to obediently follow God's leading, and leave the outcome up to Him. And we're certainly not to forsake faithfulness in our daily walk in our quest to accomplish great things for Christ.

If we become so concerned with our overarching purpose that we miss the daily call, we will be prone to a prideful attitude, one that says we're too important to take time for humble acts of service that do nothing to further our success—at least, our personal vision of success, which may not match God's.

That's a lesson Jen Ferguson learned a few months after she and her husband, Craig, launched their book *Pure Eyes, Clean Heart: A Couple's Journey to Freedom from Pornography*. At the time, Jen was also blogging and teaching women's Bible studies and planning and speaking at retreats. "Then my daughter looked at me with this sadness in her eyes," she recalled. "She needed my emotional capacity and I had nothing to give her. Nothing. It was in that moment that I knew I wasn't living in the order that I needed to. I had let my purpose in ministry to the world overshadow and overcome my purpose in ministry to my family."

It's a hard lesson for all of us. Even more important than the big-picture purpose for our lives is "the daily call to listen to God's voice and do what He says, to walk with purpose in every step," says Susie Larson in her book *Your Beautiful Purpose*. "Moreover, if we tend to the daily call, if Jesus has our full attention from day to day, moment to moment, He'll get us where we need to go so that we can live out the big-picture, divinely appointed call written over our lives."[6]

SHIFTING PRIORITIES

As each of us change and grow over the course of our lives, our individual priorities shift and evolve as well, as my friend Kristi has learned. She's worked in the counseling field for nearly twenty years, and early on, when she was obtaining her master's and doctoral degrees, her purpose was largely centered on her own goals, including her marriage. "But once I finished the PhD and we had children, I was suddenly splitting my vocational aspirations with my personal commitments," she told me. "I now teach graduate counseling students, and am the mother of three young children. Both of these fill me with great purpose. Though I consider them to hold differing value in my life, they are both significant in their impact."

Unlike Kristi, Lainna Callentine *left* a full-time career as a doctor to be a stay-at-home mom who homeschools her children. She still practices medicine for free as a missionary doctor, and says, "I'm following God's unique blueprint for my life." Life has different priorities in different seasons, Lainna says, "and the only way you can be sure of yours is to lean and stay close to God to determine the way your time should be allocated."

I believe Lainna is spot on. Our purpose and priorities should come from God's leading—and we do well to recognize that He leads His children on different paths. What is right for Kristi is different from what is right for Lainna. My life looks different from yours. We are different people, so this is only as is it should be.

Prayerfully ask God to reveal or confirm *His* purpose for you. I guarantee it will be far more valuable than counting coffee spoons. When you sense His leading, lean into His direction for your life with confidence.

According to His Purpose

Cerebral palsy. As soon as the words left the doctor's lips, Kimberly Drew's world changed forever. Until that moment, she'd thought her daughter Abbey suffered only from developmental delays. Dearly held visions that Abbey's childhood would resemble Kimberly's vanished.

"When the fog of trauma lifted, I saw God was there the whole time, and His Word promises that He is working all things for my good, but according to *His* purpose," she says.

God shaped Kimberly into the kind of woman who could carry out His purposes. "Raising Abbey has strengthened me as a person, and as a follower of Christ. I always felt called to minister to others and share the gospel—I just didn't know I would be doing that through the avenue of having children with special needs. Once I surrendered to that, it became very beautiful to me."

Kimberly had three more biological children after Abbey, one of whom is already in heaven. "I got into a pace of life that was very comfortable and was about to send my youngest to school," she told me. "This was going to mean lots of extra time to write, help at church, maybe even work outside the home. Then I found myself in a whirlwind adoption of another child—and our second with special needs—and not a stitch of money to pay for it. I had even given away all my baby stuff!"

It was overwhelming to Kimberly to imagine raising another child with a whole new set of needs, not all of which were yet discernible. Still, she asked herself: "Kimberly, you just wrote this beautiful book on the joys and blessings of raising a child with special needs.[7] Do you really believe it? Is Abbey making you a better person? If all of that was true, do you trust God to give you what you need to take care of her even though there is a good chance that this baby will be severely disabled?"

She sat down and cried, and surrendered. "I remember thinking, 'Lord, if this is the path you want us to go down, I don't know if I can do it. I think it's going to be hard, and I don't know if I have what it takes . . . but I trust you. Give me the courage to say yes.'" Kimberly clings to the promise that with God all things are possible, including her ability to care for her children the way that they need. "If time and energy are manna, then I have to come to Him every single day for my ration . . . and trust that tomorrow it will be there again."

If there were no purpose in life, Kimberly says, "I would probably be a sad statistic. Knowing that God has a purpose for everything—my pain, my pleasure, my successes and failures—changes the way I process every experience. I'm not going through my life saying, 'What does this mean?' I'm going through life saying, 'Where is God in this, how can this help me to know Him better, how does this help me to understand myself and my circumstances through the lens of my belief system?' Those answers are found in Scripture. They don't change because my life changes! Praise God He is knowable and that, while there are some mysteries of our faith, I can rest in the knowledge of God's unchanging character. Peace and security follow!"

Your Turn

1. Where do you find meaning?
2. What do you sense your big-picture purpose may be?
3. Do the priorities written on your calendar match the priorities of your heart?
4. On a scale of 1 to 10, how well do you think you're living out your daily call?
5. Where do you place your identity?

Truths to Trust

Your life has purpose.
God created you with specific good works in mind.

My gift is for you!

CHAPTER 2

Unapologetically Focused

✳ *Each of you should use whatever gift you have received to serve others, as faithful stewards of God's grace in its various forms.*

1 PETER 4:10

I want a singleness of eye, a purity of intention, a central core to my life that will enable me to carry out these obligations and activities as well as I can. . . . I would like to achieve a state of inner spiritual grace from which I could function and give as I was meant to in the eye of God.

ANNE MORROW LINDBERGH
Gift from the Sea

M y grip tightened on the phone I held to my ear. For a moment, I was too stunned to respond.

I had just explained to a woman that my existing commitments prevented me from accepting a position on the board of directors for a local girls' organization. I didn't expect her to be happy about it. But I didn't expect her to say what she said, either.

"Excuse me?" I managed to squeak out.

"I said I forgive you," the voice on the other end of the line repeated. "I forgive you for this, because Jesus forgave me for my sins."

Hmm.

Usually, I'm a sucker for false guilt, but that comment did not work on me.

Can you and I agree on something right now? *It is not a sin to know and communicate our limits.* It is not a sin to prioritize and make choices that best align with God's purpose for ourselves and for the health of our families. If you only remember one thing from this chapter, let this be it.

God doesn't require us to say yes to every request for our time and energy. Consider the words of Jesus in Luke 14:28. "Suppose one of you wants to build a tower. Won't you first sit down and estimate the cost to see if you have enough money to complete it?" Before adding another commitment to our lives, the responsible thing is to calculate whether we have the resources to see it through. And our available resources, including time and energy, will always depend on our current season.

LIFE BY THE SEASONS

Living by seasons is something native Alaskans understand very well. If you've ever been to "The Last Frontier" in summer *not load hearing creatures)*

not donkeys but we are sheep

or winter, you've experienced the extreme nature of its seasons. During the summer, the sun barely blinks its blazing eye. In winter, the nights stretch out long.

When I lived there myself, these seasons on steroids felt unnatural to me—so I fought against them. In the summer, I taped tinfoil over our bedroom windows to block the light. When that wasn't enough, I added black garbage bags, all impulses toward an HGTV-inspired home bowing to my need for sleep. I'm still not sure if it was the insomnia of those summer months or my efforts to fight nature that made me a little crazy.

The winter I spent in Alaska, from October to March, was so dark. And with the darkness came this irresistible urge to sleep from evening to mid-morning. That felt wrong to me, too, so with Rob away on his Coast Guard cutter somewhere in the Bering Sea, I would turn on all the lights in the house and flip on the television, just to have some noise. I was fighting to stay awake, because that's what I thought a normal person should do.

At some point during my year there, a woman who had lived in Alaska her whole life gently told me I was doing it all wrong. "You have to live by the seasons," she told me. "During the summer months, enjoy the sunshine! You know it won't last long. Stay outside and soak it in. Have a mocha at midnight. Talk with friends on the beach and don't bother checking to see if it's bedtime yet."

In the winter, she told me, people tend to hibernate, staying home during the dark evenings and reading by the fire until they feel like sleeping. Most of them spend so much energy on seasonal work in the summertime—things like fishing and tourism—that winter is a welcome respite.

Many of them have some sort of artistic hobby, whether pottery or painting or wood carving, that they pursue in the dark months. And when they're tired, they sleep. Their bodies catch up from the rest they missed in the summer. "When your body can harmonize with the seasons here," my friend said, "life will be much better."

Since then, this lesson has taken root in my mind in a deeper way. When we live fully in the season in which we find ourselves, we find peace. As we lean into God's calling for our lives, we recognize that our seasons affect how we do that. Navigating a new job, parenting small children, guiding teens through adolescence, grieving the loss of a loved one or of a dream—these and countless other life events thrust us into different seasons of varying lengths of time. As Bruce Miller writes, "Burnout comes from trying to seize opportunities that do not fit the current season of your life; it is created by trying to meet unreleased false expectations."[1]

THE FREEDOM TO FOCUS

When we recognize which season we're in, we can more easily see the most pressing work laid out for us, as well as the tasks that don't fit within this frame. Understanding that our work was prepared in advance for us to do (Ephesians 2:10), and that we are to work at it with all our heart (Colossians 3:23), we can be confident in focusing our energies.

First Peter 4:10–11 tells us, "Each of you should use whatever gift you have received to serve others, as faithful stewards of God's grace in its various forms. If anyone speaks, they should do so as one who speaks the very words of God.

I Corinthians 12:4

If anyone serves, they should do so with the strength God provides, so that in all things God may be praised through Jesus Christ."

Did you see that? We get to use our own gifts, not someone else's. Take a few moments to read 1 Corinthians 12, and you'll notice what pains the apostle Paul takes to clarify that the body of Christ works for one purpose—God's glory—even as we all have different roles to play. The one who is gifted with teaching should teach, not prophesy or speak in tongues.

This passage is likely already familiar to many of us. We nod our heads to the principle of each person using her own spiritual gift. But it doesn't always carry over into the other areas of our lives.

We are better together ←

OWN YOUR STRENGTHS

A few years ago, while speaking to a group of educators, I shared how grateful I am for my English teachers who had noticed my ability to write and encouraged me to nurture that skill. Afterward, a teacher came up to me, saying, "You said your teachers told you to do more of what you're good at."

"That's right," I replied. I wondered why she looked so confused.

"But that flies in the face of everything we've been taught as educators," she said. "We have always been told to find the student's weaknesses and focus on those." The teacher took a step back. "This is radically different from what I've been doing. This changes everything."

Her experience reflects a cultural norm. When American young people ages eighteen to twenty-five were asked whether building on their strengths or fixing their weaknesses would help them most in life, 70 percent chose the latter.[2] "Yet, lastingly successful people . . . focus on their strengths," says Marcus Buckingham, an authority on strengths-based management and leadership in the workforce. "A weakness is an activity that weakens you, even if you're good at it," he says. "A strength is an activity that strengthens you."[3]

In the workplace, Buckingham's company found that "most employees are not even trying to use their strengths at work. Our Strengths Confidence Index shows that only 41 percent said they would achieve the most by building on their strengths, while 59 percent said fixing their weaknesses. This data suggests that most people take their strengths for granted, and instead devote most of their energies to the uphill battle of fixing their weaknesses."[4]

Buckingham's research shows what the Bible has been telling us all along: we are most effective when we focus on what God created us to do. When we identify our strengths and build on them, we're faithful stewards of what He's given us. To forsake our gifts in order to spend time and energy in areas of weakness sets us up for disappointment and ineffectiveness. *It is not selfish to use our gifts.* We serve the world best when we give what we're best at.

And yet how many times have we tried to take on a responsibility outside our calling or outside our particular season because we felt it was expected of us?

SHEDDING EXPECTATIONS

As a natural people-pleaser, my friend Sarah Sundin, a pharmacist and novelist, used to have a problem saying no. "If someone asked, I said yes," she told me. "As a result, this craft-impaired woman ended up on the MOPS crafts committee. Not a good fit. When I started writing, that had to change. Opportunities that align with my main purposes receive serious consideration. Those that don't receive an immediate no." If anyone tries to make Sarah feel guilty, she reminds herself that she is not the solution to another person's problem. "Having a clear sense of purpose helps me not feel guilty about not doing more. I know I'm doing what God wants me to do—not what people want me to do."

Sarah's final statement echoes something the apostle Paul said in his letter to the Galatians. "Am I now trying to win the approval of human beings, or of God? Or am I trying to please people? If I were still trying to please people, I would not be a servant of Christ" (1:10). Serving Christ means *His* purpose in our life takes precedence.

Australian author Bronnie Ware wrote *The Top Five Regrets of the Dying* based on her years of work in palliative care. From those nearing life's end, the regret she heard most often was, "I wish I'd had the courage to live a life true to myself, not the life others expected of me." As believers, our goal should be to live a life that is true to God's plan for us, not simply "true to ourselves." But a note of caution still rings clear in the regret Ware recorded. If we don't know what our God-given purpose is, others will be sure to impose their own purposes on us, whether they realize they're doing it or not.

I've appreciated getting to know Sarah Hamaker as a fellow member of a professional writers and speakers association. Also a parent coach, she frequently addresses "letting go of guilt and living the life God has given you right this moment." Guilt, she says, comes from unrealistic expectations. "Women tend to live their lives according to what they perceive as the expectations of others. In other words, women, especially mothers, live to fulfill others' expectations of what their life should be. Contentment is part of the equation, but what we perceive as societal expectations does more damage than lack of contentment."

Sundin rejoices in the fact that God created us to be different. "We shouldn't feel bad because we aren't good at something or don't have time to pursue all things—nor should we shame anyone who doesn't share our gifts and interests. One woman finds fulfillment in crafts, one in running the PTA, one in homeschooling, one as a lawyer . . . and I find it in writing. God did not create me to run the PTA, so I don't feel guilty about saying no to that. In fact, I would ruin the PTA through incompetence. They're better off without me. We're all good at different things, and we need each other."

FEMININE NORMS?

In a US study on conformity to feminine norms, researchers listed the most important attributes associated with "being feminine" as "being nice, pursuing a thin body ideal, showing modesty by not calling attention to one's talents or abilities, being domestic, caring for children, investing in a romantic relationship, keeping sexual intimacy contained within one committed relationship, and using our resources to invest in our appearance."[5]

If you're rolling your eyes about now, I'm right there with you, sister. It's disturbing to me, too.

And yet, oh so enlightening. The need for this chapter—indeed, for this entire book—is clear when we reflect on the first and third attributes in that list of "most important feminine norms." What's the most common reason we tend to say yes to things we're not exactly passionate about? We want to please others—or, at the very least, we don't want to disappoint them. In other words, we want to be nice. And why don't we more often simply say, "I'm good at this particular skill, this activity energizes me . . . so *this* is what I'm investing in"? Maybe, just maybe, we have bought into the idea that "calling attention to one's talents or abilities" is not what "good" women do.

When we allow these undercurrents to induce guilt, to make us do just any work that's asked of us instead of our best, we're shortchanging what God calls us to be. We're shackling our ability to lean into our purpose.

I know, because I've done it. Or rather, I almost did, had it not been for a little intervention.

One summer, I agreed to take on a three-hours-a-week commitment for the coming school year. But before long, the weekly time required tripled as my role shifted from "helper" to "leader"—in an area I know nothing about. My stress level soared as I foresaw doom: not only would I let down the people I was now expected to lead, I would spend so much time on that failure that I would also miss this book deadline.

My right eyelid twitched. My left arm hurt. When my brother emailed to ask if I could watch my nieces for ninety minutes, I shut my laptop without responding right away, unable to manage "one more request on my time."

Pay attention to signs like these. My body was protesting, and I was too overwhelmed to help my own family—the daily call to serve those closest to me. And now, I wasn't hon-oring my big-picture purpose—my writing commitments—either. Not cool.

Enter the voice of reason, named Rob. "Don't do this," he said. "You don't have time for this."

"But I said yes already!" I cried.

"No," he replied. "You said yes to three hours a week. Not to this. And if you're stressed, I'll be stressed, and I can't help you." Let the record show that Rob was working full time *and* going to grad school full time . . . so when he said he couldn't help me, he really couldn't help me. There would be no watching of kids in the evenings or on the weekends so I could write. If I was going to finish this book, I had to carve out time to do it on my own.

"But, if I say I have a book to write, doesn't that sound like I think my busyness is more important than their busy-ness?" (Insert hand-wringing here.)

Rob gaped at me. "You *do* have a book to write. They can take it however they want to take it, but that's the truth."

He was right, of course. There had been a time, a year earlier, when I was between book contracts and I'd invested more heavily in my community. But for this particular season, Rob and I were both nose-to-the-grindstone so we could accomplish our projects and still maintain a healthy family life. One thing I've learned—if the timing is wrong, nothing can make it right. If it doesn't fit into your current season, if you don't have the resources of time and energy to see it through, that's a guilt-free *no*.

I declined that nine-hour weekly commitment so I could write and still have time for my family—and this time no one accused me of sinning. Hallelujah.

LET OTHERS SERVE

Perhaps you feel overwhelmed with what others require of you, too. Some of my closest friends and relatives are pastors' wives, who seem to shoulder a particularly heavy burden in this area. When I talked to Michelle Lazurek, a pastor's wife and life coach, she told me, "A pastor's wife first needs not to feel pressured to fill the shoes of the previous pastor's wife, despite how much the church would want her to."

"Secondly," Michelle added, "she needs to figure out how God has gifted her and stick within her gifting. Thirdly, if no one else is going to do a ministry and it is in danger of dying—*let it die.* Everything has a season, even ministries. Perhaps God is allowing something to die to make room for a new ministry."

This is a lesson that applies to all of us. Fear—that no one else will take on a task if we don't—is not an adequate reason to add that responsibility to your life. Taking on a role because it's expected of us, without regard for our own strengths or weaknesses, isn't a good enough reason, either.

"A church member once asked me to do a part of Vacation Bible School," Michelle recalls. "She said, 'No pressure, but the last pastor's wife did it.' I am not a children's teacher, but I didn't know how to say no, so I agreed. And I was miserable! After VBS was over, I expressed to the church member my hesitance to do it again. She replied, 'You didn't seem like you wanted to do it anyway.' Needless to say, I have not done VBS since then."

This story gives us a glimpse into an uncomfortable truth. We don't want to let people down by saying no, but we can still let them down by saying yes. If an opportunity doesn't align with our gifts, our purpose, and our resources, it's not just better for us but it's better for *others* to let some-one else fill the role.

Catherine Fitzgerald learned this the hard way. A mili-tary wife I've known for several years, she contributed to one of my earlier books. Recently, she was stressed by the amount of time she was giving to church and nonprofit organizations when she really wanted and needed to be a homeschooling mom. "Relationships were out of whack," Catherine told me, "because I was bone dry after all my various commitments, and my time with the Lord was less and less." But ultimately, she says, she was able to "untangle the web." God showed Catherine that "nothing is dependent on me. Ministries will go on, other people will step up. The only unique roles I have are mama and wife, so my first order of business is time with the Lord and then my family. God will show me my 'yeses' for the rest. Being focused instead of divided is essential to complete the work He has for me."

"TORN-TO-PIECES-HOOD"

When our energies are spread too thin, we feel it. "Like butter that has been scraped over too much bread," says Bilbo Baggins in Tolkien's *The Fellowship of the Ring*. There's a German word, *zerrissenheit*, that describes the feeling—it implies "brokenness" or "inner conflict," but was colorfully translated as "torn-to-pieces-hood" by the psychologist and philosopher William James. I totally get that. I don't mind giving myself to purposeful work, but when pulled in too many directions at once, I feel torn to pieces.

Anne Morrow Lindbergh, the American aviation pioneer who raised five children after the kidnapping and murder of her firstborn, contemplated women's patterns of living in her groundbreaking 1955 book *Gift from the Sea*. "Woman instinctively wants to give, yet resents giving herself in small pieces," she wrote. "I believe that what woman resents is not so much giving herself in pieces as giving herself purposelessly. What we fear is not so much that our energy may be leaking away through small outlets as that it may be going 'down the drain.'... Purposeful giving is not as apt to deplete one's resources; it belongs to that natural order of giving that seems to renew itself even in the act of depletion."[6]

This, then, is the heart of the matter. We must invest ourselves purposefully or end up in a state of "torn-to-pieces-hood."

My friend Shannon Popkin and I love swapping stories on this topic when we see each other. Like me, she finds both purpose and freedom in Ephesians 2:10. "That verse says that I am God's workmanship—so He fashioned me in a particular way—and that He has particular assignments, prepared in advance, with my name on them," she told me. "I was designed to serve Jesus in a particular way! So I won't have time to serve Him in *all* ways, which is freeing."

After serving in her church, family, and community for decades, Shannon has grown more selective in how she invests her time. "I've experimented enough to know how I'm gifted and how I'm not, and I try to prioritize serving in the ways I am most uniquely gifted," she says. "In recent years, God has opened doors for me to write, speak, and teach the Bible to women. But in order to do those things, I can't serve in some of the ways I used to."

She once felt guilty about that, because of what others may have thought. "In truth," she says now, "we need only do what God has assigned us—anything more will bog down our schedules and keep us from the 'good works prepared in advance for us to do.'"

NOT EVERYTHING BLOOMS AT ONCE

One of the most meaningful things I've learned about seasons and focus came from a wordless source—my garden. Planted almost exclusively with perennials, it displays a comforting truth so simple that it's easy to miss: not everything blooms at once. Isn't this true in life as well? As my grandmother has reminded me, "Life is long, and has many parts."

Put another way, not everything belongs in the same season, and that's okay. "Some of our insane busyness in life comes from trying to cultivate, plant, fertilize, harvest, and repair the fences in every season," writes Bruce Miller. "We are not meant to live that way."[7] God created seasons, and we are free to focus on one at a time.

When author and freelance writer PeggySue Wells heard that I was working on this book, she jumped at the chance to share her perspective as a single, working mother of seven. She told me, "I do it all, but not all at the same time. I'm thankful for the four seasons and for seasons in life." Now that most of her kids are out of the house, PeggySue no longer gardens and cans. She also invests one day to make and freeze thirty meals, listens to audio books in the car, and hires teenagers to do basic housekeeping and yard work around her five acres, all to free up time to focus on her job.

"The list of what I *don't* do is as important as what I do," she adds. "I never sew since I can't and maintain my salvation. Christmas cards are on my 'don't do' list, though I like to receive them. Instead of a Christmas tree, we set up a large nativity set and place gifts around the base."

As I write this in Iowa, it's autumn. My black-eyed Susans have dropped their bright orange petals, leaving only stiff stalks to rattle in the strengthening wind. The rich purple plumes of my salvia plants have faded into memory, but my burning bush is ablaze with flaming red leaves. Grey-bellied clouds and a bite in the air tell me that soon, snow will throw its blanket over everything. This, too, is a lesson: our seasons are temporary. May we enjoy them as much as we can before they slip away.

FOCUS ON WHOLENESS

For most of this chapter, we've viewed *focus* as directing our energies toward production or output of some kind. We've talked about the importance of matching our outside commitments and resources to our gifts and purpose. But wholeness cannot be achieved by simple time management, even if everything in our schedule aligns with our calling.

In *Rhythms of Grace*, Kerri Weems shares her habit of countering an overwhelmed spirit by purchasing a new calendar or day planner and sitting down at Starbucks to write all her tasks neatly in the grid before her, a visual roadmap of how she will accomplish all her work. On one of these occasions, she realized, "The better my life management systems were, the more productive I could be. But . . . my tactics would never lead to the peace and wholeness I was looking for. Is it any wonder that, for all of my organizing and systematizing, my world still felt chaotic?"[8]

What Kerri discovered was this: "I experience shalom when I focus on wholeness, not productivity." She defines *shalom*, simply speaking, as wholeness, an inner peace, or "the way things are supposed to be."[9]

We are far from experiencing shalom when we sign up for things out of guilt and have little time left over for our purpose. These are the types of decisions we can control.

The reality of life, however, is that it is often more complicated than just saying no. What of the mom who would love more time with her children but feels equally called to her career—or must work just to pay the bills? What of the woman who pours herself into caregiving until she has nothing left? These situations and countless others necessarily fracture our energy. Must our hearts also be fractured as well?

Psalm 147:3 says the Lord "heals the brokenhearted and binds up their wounds." Through God's grace and your own focused care on spiritual well-being, wholeness of heart is still possible.

My friend Rebekah Benimoff juggles care for three people with medical needs—her husband was diagnosed with PTSD, her teenaged son is dealing with diabetes, and her youngest son has sensory needs. "As a recovering 'people pleaser,' it can be hard to say no, as I simply hate to disappoint—but time for us to rest and recover is key," she says. "Self-care for the caregiver is imperative. Anything that would take away from our recovery time has to be cut, even if someone gets offended." Rebekah says she's in a continual process of accepting the fact that it is not her job to make everyone happy—though it is her job to advocate for her family and herself. "I take better care of my family's needs when I take care of my needs, as well."

It may be tempting to skip the invisible but important care of our own hearts and minds. But we can only do what we are made to do if we also focus on wholeness—who we were made to *be*.

The apostle Paul tells us not to be conformed to the world's ways, but to be transformed by the renewing of our minds (Romans 12:2). The way to renew our minds is through prayer and meditating on God's Word. Take a look at this: "All Scripture is God-breathed and is useful for teaching, rebuking, correcting and training in righteousness, so that the servant of God may be thoroughly equipped for every good work" (2 Timothy 3:16–17). What is the purpose of God's Word? To equip us for *every good work.*

Even the busiest person, the most time-starved and torn-to-pieces among us can begin to meditate on Scripture, one verse at a time. John Ortberg spells out how:

Take, for example, this thought from Psalm 46:10: "Be still, and know that I am God!" For one day, live with these words. Let your mind continually return to them in secret:

"Today, as best as I can, I am going to be still. I am not going to chatter thoughtlessly. I will remember that I don't have to defend myself or make sure people think of me the way I want them to. Today I don't have to get my way. Today, before I make decisions, I will try to listen for God's voice. Today I am not going to be tossed around by anxiety or anger—I will take those feelings as prompts from the Spirit to listen first. In each of these situations I will ask God, 'How would you like me to respond?' I will live in stillness."[10]

Focusing on who we are (and *whose* we are) must come before we focus on what we do.

Maybe you feel so sliced and diced you can't imagine experiencing wholeness. Maybe exhaustion makes it hard for you even to finish this chapter, despite your best intentions. If so, hear these words from Susie Larson: "It's not wrong to be tired. It's not wrong to feel overwhelmed. It's not wrong to go through seasons of complete chaos. What is wrong—and heartbreakingly foolish and wonderfully avoidable—is to live a life with more craziness than we want because we have less of Jesus than we need."[11]

Be still, dear woman, and know that He is God. Take a breath. As you focus on your priorities, trust that the God who created the universe from the void can bring order to your heart and life.

*Find true North

Free to Focus

At the age of eighteen, while in college, Dianne Barker landed her dream job: writing for the local newspaper. By the time she was twenty-four, she'd written her first book. Later, her 1986 release *Twice Pardoned* was the first book for Focus on the Family Publishing—and a number one Christian best seller.

"After that," says Dianne, "the Lord gradually led me away from my very public life as journalist, speaker, and best-selling author to what I call a 'shrunken life'—taking care of my parents and my husband's parents as they declined in health and getting our two kids through high school and college."

She grocery shopped and cooked for her family of four, her parents, and her parents-in-law; drove everyone to medical appointments; and did laundry for three families. "One week I washed thirty-two loads at the coin laundry due to plumbing problems at our house," she recalls. "I gave up everything except attending church and school functions involving our kids. I had no time, energy, or focus for anything else. If my life had eternal significance, I needed to invest it passionately, making the most of the talents the Lord gave me."

Paul's instruction 2 Timothy 2:4 offered a helpful perspective. "As a soldier must remain focused, I needed to eliminate even some good activities that entangled," Dianne says. "I learned to say no to some opportunities without guilt, knowing someone else could do those tasks. No one else could rear my children and care for our parents or write the message God had given me."

Still, at first she felt baffled. "After clarifying my calling to write, God had taken me off the public stage, shrinking my life little by little. Although I never resisted the caregiving and gladly served our parents, I fought frustration over a book I'd started but hadn't finished and humiliation when anyone asked about it. One day as I wrestled with God about this, He spoke in my heart. *You're in this place by my design. Someday I will enlarge your life again.* I felt immediate peace. Accepting the circumstance lifted the pressure. I couldn't do it all—but I wanted to do this assignment well and, looking back, have no regrets. We buried three parents in five years and continued caring for my father-in-law another eight years. The peace stayed, and the promise carried me through many exhausting days. During those many years in His waiting room, I knew He was doing something bigger than I could see."

In 2001, after her parents were in heaven and her kids had left home to pursue advanced degrees, Dianne began reinventing herself by attending writing conferences. By this time, she'd been out of the publishing world for fifteen years. "The Lord began enlarging my life, just as He'd promised," she says. She published magazine articles, guest blog posts, and self-published two books. God even surprised her with a weekly radio program on a Christian station in Bristol, Tennessee.

"My sole desire is that my life count for God," Dianne says. "While struggling to say no to other commitments in order to give my writing priority, I found this verse: 'I am doing a great work, so that I cannot come down: why should the work cease, whilst I leave it, and come down to you?' (Nehemiah 6:3 KJV). God had called Nehemiah to rebuild the wall around Jerusalem. Giving the work priority meant saying no to other distractions. I printed that verse and put it on my desk, where it remains today. It helps me say no without guilt."

Your Turn

1. How does guilt affect your ability to prioritize?
2. How would you describe the season you're in right now?
3. Is there anything you're trying to do in this season that would fit better in a different season? How can you make adjustments for that?
4. When you feel torn to pieces, how do you focus on wholeness?
5. How can you spend more time building on your strengths rather than trying to fix weaknesses or serve from those lesser places?

Truths to Trust

Prioritizing your time is not a sin.
Using your gifts honors God.

CHAPTER 3

The Myth of Measuring Up

Differing weights and differing measures—
the LORD detests them both.

PROVERBS 20:10

We gain nothing by committing the sin of comparison.
In fact, it only bears two kinds of fruit—pride or despair—
neither of which come from the Vine.

SUSIE LARSON
Your Beautiful Purpose

When I was in my early twenties, my then-boyfriend pointed to a magazine cover portraying a flawlessly airbrushed celebrity and asked, "Do you think you could look more like that?" Yes, he was serious. (I made sure to ask.) No, I didn't marry him.

As much as that bothered me, though, it didn't hold a candle to how I felt during Mom's Night at my son's school a few years ago. In preparation for the event, teachers had asked each child what his or her mom was the very best at, then made a poster showing their answers.

I braced myself, recalling that two years earlier, my daughter's answer was "makes refrigerated crescent rolls." But I went ahead and read down the list of warm-fuzzy answers of the "plays board games with me," "makes ice cream out of snow," and "takes me to Disney World" variety. And then there was Ethan's answer, in large, accusing letters:

STARTS UP MY VIDEO GAME

Oh. For. The love.

My face burned with humiliation as I sat criss-cross applesauce on the alphabet-patterned carpet. I couldn't tell which was worse, the judgment I imagined coming from the teachers and other moms in the room, or the condemnation rising up within myself. Being compared to a magazine model had nothing on this—trying to live up to a room full of other moms who clearly had their ever-loving acts together.

The truth was, I did most of the other mom-things on that poster, too. Along with Rob, I also made family dinner time a well-protected priority. And Bible reading at bedtime. And, yes, I turned on Super Mario Brothers.

Comparison is a beast, isn't it? And not one of us escapes its bite.

CONFORM AND COMPETE

In *The Gifts of Imperfection*, researcher Brené Brown says that when we start comparing ourselves with others, "we want to see who or what is best out of a specific collection of 'alike things.' . . . We don't compare our houses to the mansions across town; we compare our yard to the yards on our block. When we compare, we want to be the best or have the best of our group. The comparison mandate becomes this crushing paradox of 'fit in and stand out!' It's not cultivate self-acceptance, belonging, and authenticity; it's be just like everyone else, but better."[1]

How exhausting. Part of the trouble is that we're so good at comparing, much of the time we don't even realize we're doing it. It becomes automatic. I can be feeling fine until I read on Facebook that another author has written twenty-four pages in one day *while having the flu*. Suddenly, I'm grumpy. Why? Because in a split second, I've put my paltry word count for the day on a scale with this other author's colossal work—and I've come up short. I'm no longer at peace with my own capacity, despite the fact that I deliberately chose to set my work aside to spend time playing bingo with my kids.

When we compare, we assign value to one experience (or life), judging it to be better than another. This is not our place. We don't know God's purpose for another woman's life. We don't know the trials she has had to overcome, or her blessings or sufferings, or her current season in life. In other words, comparison is futile because we will always be using differing weights and measures.

My friend Kimberly Spragg and I once worked at the same nonprofit higher education association in Washington, DC. Now, she's an off-campus student program director in Australia, and admits that she compares herself to others all the time. "There are times I feel like I'm not doing all that I could be," she told me. "At the same time, I also struggle with sometimes feeling like I am better at my job than others. I have times of insecurity and times of pride. Both are very dangerous, I think. We can't compare our issues, our role, our gifts to others. I know when I've done a good job and I also know when I've been lazy. I need to stick with that and not compare myself to others."

The English Standard Version of the Bible translates Proverbs 11:1 this way: "A false balance is an abomination to the LORD, but a just weight is his delight." In those days, silver was weighed on scales balanced against a stone weight. Weights with dishonest labels were used for cheating. Comparison is a dishonest label, too, cheating us out of peace, joy, and contentment.

RELEASING THE BURDEN

Though Proverbs 4:25–27 exhorts us to look neither to the right nor to the left, we rarely walk through life wearing blinders. If we're not careful, we'll even compare our weaknesses—those areas that drain us, which we have chosen not to focus on—to other women's strengths. Talk about differing weights and measures! Yet each time we stumble in this area is an opportunity to refresh our perspective. Listen as five women share how:

Sarah Sundin: When my oldest son was born, I made the transition from full-time pharmacist to stay-at-home mom. I didn't fit in. All the stay-at-home moms did crafts and homeschooled. I believed I could best train my children to be "in the world but not of the world" by placing them in public school and being actively involved in their education. However, to overcome this serious "mom-deficiency," I decided to try crafts. I have the glue gun burns and some hideous creations to prove it. I felt like a failure as a mom, even though my children were thriving. How silly is that?

In time, I found other moms with similar interests. More importantly, I found moms with different interests who didn't feel that all moms had to do exactly what they did. I became comfortable in my own skin, with my own talents (or lack thereof), and with the decisions my husband and I had made prayerfully.

Colleen: As a caregiver to my veteran husband, I am very connected to that community. I see different caregivers going out and conquering the world, or getting straight A's in college (I am *still* plugging away at my bachelor's degree) and I question myself—I wonder why I am not achieving the same things. At times, it makes me sarcastic and biting. I have spent years working on coming to the place where, when I feel those things rising up in me, *not* to speak or address the people around me but to first look inside and see why I am feeling that way. In this life, it's very easy to be bitter, but I refuse to allow bitterness to control me.

Cara: I often feel like I'm not saving my best for my son. I feel that maybe he should be involved in more things, but when would I take him? Sports are in the evenings, when I teach violin. I see a lot of parents whose lives revolve around their kids. I would like to be something like that but it's not feasible. I have to work. And because I'm divorced, my time with my son is even more limited because, of course, he spends time with his dad, too.

I finally realized it's okay, because when we do have time together, I make sure he knows he's a priority. We plan family vacations now, and when we have weekends together they're sacred. We do intentional and loving faith-based things that I wouldn't push for as much if I was with him all the time.

Ann: I compare myself fairly often. For example, I have a friend whose gift is hospitality. She loves to have people over, she's made boatloads of food, her house is always clean and beautifully decorated—and worse, her kids didn't like to come to *our* house because it wasn't clean enough. I can become a quivering mess about this because if someone stopped over at my house unannounced, they would find it decidedly imperfect. So I usually say no to having people over.

But I realized that hospitality takes many forms. I never minded having neighborhood kids over; I invite people over for a backyard picnic once in a while; I'm welcoming and friendly in other social settings; I focus more on people than on a perfect house.

Jenny: When I'm not consistent in prayer, Scripture reading, and quiet time with the Lord, I take my eyes off Him and His purpose for my life and start looking at others. The woman with a thriving ministry at church. The mom that homeschools twice as many children as me. The friend whose house is always impeccable. Yet when I'm resting in who God created me to be and where He has placed me—and walking in obedience to what He has called me to do—there is joy and contentment and peace.

Each of these women gained fresh insight on what it means to be a person who lives faithful to her purpose—and what it doesn't mean. There is such freedom to be gained in releasing what we were never meant to carry.

UNFAIR COMPARISONS

When I studied in England for a month, some friends and I took a weekend to visit Paris. We arrived so early in the morning that it was still dark. After a few quiet minutes of looking out the train window, my friend Erin spoke up.

"Well I'm disappointed," she said. "So far it looks a lot like Cleveland."

The comparison is so funny to me (no offense, Cleveland—go, Indians) because it was made in the dark.

Actually, comparing in the dark is pretty common. What I mean is this: It's human nature to draw quick conclusions about ourselves and others, even when we can't see the whole picture—such as when we're on social media. And, sadly, our conclusions usually aren't favorable to ourselves. The research backs this up:

- A University of Michigan study shows that the more time people spent on Facebook, the more their overall satisfaction declined. They felt sadder and lonelier.
- An analysis of forty studies confirms that Internet use had a negative effect on overall well-being. One experiment concluded that Facebook increased feelings of jealousy, thereby causing relational problems.
- Researchers from Berlin found that the more time people spent browsing Facebook, as opposed to engaging with their Facebook "friends" or creating content, the more envious they felt. A Carnegie Mellon study drew the same conclusion.

The envy these study participants felt was "further exacerbated by a general similarity of people's social networks to themselves: because the point of comparison is like-minded peers, learning about the achievements of others hits even harder."[2]

To be clear: using Facebook to *actively* engage with friends and community can be encouraging. But when we simply scroll through passively, we gain nothing. Comparing our real lives to the carefully selected images and updates on Facebook is not a fair comparison at all. When we measure other people's highlight reels to our own ordinary and stressful days, we're on a slippery slope to jealousy. If we aren't careful, scrolling through social media can leave us feeling "less than."

When PeggySue Wells sees posts by other professionals in her field, especially people of her own age, she will compare their productivity with hers, and worry over "how they appear to be rooted in the center of God's abundant calling." Then, she says, she begins feeling not only like "a slacker" but that "I'm outside the train of life that is flying by filled with all the smart people who knew how to get aboard while I am still looking for the place to purchase a ticket."

Likewise, author and illustrator Ann-Margret Hovsepian told me, "I used to feel resentful that writers a lot younger than me seemed to be achieving success a lot faster than I have over the last twenty years, partly because they've started their careers in the era of social media and they know how to make good use of it. But I've realized that it's okay that my journey was slower. It has shaped who I am and, I hope, earned me credibility that can only come over a long period of time. As long as I'm doing *my* best, it's okay if I'm not *the* best."

Studies show that Instagram is even more depressing than Facebook; the more time we spend looking at other people's picture-perfect moments, the more dissatisfied we'll feel with the ordinary, unglamorous moments that make up most of our real lives.[3] And in a *Today* survey of seven thousand US mothers, 42 percent said that they sometimes suffer from "Pinterest stress"—the worry that they're not crafty or creative enough.[4]

Even Joanna Gaines, star of the hit HGTV show *Fixer Upper*, has felt "less than" after scrolling through social media. "As a stay-at-home mom, every time I had a moment to open Facebook or Pinterest I would walk away thinking, I'm not doing enough," she said. "And then I'd start second-guessing myself."[5] She has since overcome this feeling, but if Joanna Gaines isn't immune to these feelings, who is?

My friend Jenny told me something that really benefited my own perspective. "It's helpful to remember that the woman who does all the amazing homeschool activities may have a messy house or may always be behind on laundry. I think our blogging/social media culture has made it so easy for people to put their 'best' on display. Then we look at other women's 'bests' and think we need to do it all—Pinterest crafts, ministries at church, gourmet meals, stellar home-schooling, immaculate house, and so on. We don't."

Even those of us who don't pin, post, tweet, or snap can become discouraged by comparison. And sometimes the most unrelenting, unforgiving standard is the one we set for ourselves.

COMPARED TO THE ME I WISH I WERE

One of my closest friends from college, Maria, works in part-time youth ministry and is the mother of three young children, including a daughter with Angelman syndrome, a complex genetic disorder. "I feel frustrated at times that

I don't have time or the capacity to do a lot of the things I see other moms and kids on social media doing," she told me. "But I mainly struggle with comparing my actual life to my personal standards. I don't care what other people think of my house, but I personally would love less clutter, more clean. Other people think I'm a great mom, but I think I should spend more time playing with my kids than I do." Maria keeps a "grief journal" to help her process her sad feelings and move forward.

Taking note of those times when we feel most vulnerable to comparisons, whether to each other or to "the me I could be," is the first step to minimizing the power they hold over us. Cynthia, an English professor and writer friend of mine, says, "I'm convinced that much of mental health and spiritual health is managing the Critic that I hear often (or maybe *always*) in my head. I often feel like I'm not measuring up. The college where I teach is small—it isn't Harvard. A publisher hasn't yet agreed to publish my novel. I weigh more than I ever have. And on and on this needling voice pricks me." But Cynthia has found encouragement from a friend, a recovering alcoholic, who taught her the acronym HALT. "An alcoholic lets this acronym remind her that when she's Hungry, Angry, Lonely, or Tired, watch out," Cynthia told me. "She has to be extra cautious regarding what prompts her. This is good advice for us all."

My friend and former colleague Amber worked full time as a university's director of communications both when she was pregnant and now that she parents two small children. She told me, "I am 'doing it all,' but I'm certainly not doing any of it to the level I'd be capable of hitting if I were only focused on a few of the things instead of all of the things." Amber estimates she's giving 85 percent of the effort she'd ideally like to give at work, and her house is normally at about 60 percent of the level of tidiness that she'd like.

"My comparison is not even to celebrities or mythical soccer moms," she says, "it's a comparison to what I know I *could* do if I could just focus and get through life on more than five hours of sleep. I'm most vulnerable to this feeling when I'm tired or frustrated, and it's killer. I'm so grateful for every bit of my life . . . but I still compare myself to who I thought I'd be instead of who I am."

Don't we all do this? Don't we all judge ourselves according to what we think we could do and be on our very best day, if there were no distractions or limitations on our time or health or motivation? And yet, I cringe to say it, that day will never come—which makes this another unfair comparison.

WORDS FROM AN ASPIRING GOOD-ENOUGHIST

There is a difference between striving to be our best and perfectionism, says Brené Brown, a self-proclaimed "recovering perfectionist and aspiring good-enoughist." Rather than being about healthy achievement and growth, Brown says, "Perfectionism is, at its core, about trying to earn approval and acceptance."[6]

Ironically, research shows that perfectionism actually hampers success. It often leads to depression, anxiety, addiction, and life-paralysis. "Perfectionism is self-destructive simply because there is no such thing as perfect," says Brown. "When we become more loving and compassionate with ourselves and we begin to practice shame resilience, we can embrace our imperfections. It is in the process of embracing our imperfections that we find our truest gifts: courage, compassion, and connection."[7]

God doesn't call us to be perfect people. He calls us to be faithful, obedient, loving, just, merciful. He calls us to rely on Him. As God said to the apostle Paul, "My grace is sufficient for you, for my power is made perfect in weakness." And that is why Paul could say, "I will boast all the more gladly about my weaknesses, so that Christ's power may rest on me" (2 Corinthians 12:9).

Experiencing stress and conflict does not necessarily mean we're doing life "wrong." Jesus told us that we would have trouble in this world (John 16:33), and here on earth, Christ himself, the Prince of Peace, did not lead a life that was free from hardship and stress. But we do get to tap into an all-sufficient, supernatural grace and a peace that defies understanding. We also get hope. As Amber says about the stressful stage of life she's in, "It's not forever—it's just for now."

Hope is more than a feeling or emotion. Borrowing from the work of C. R. Snyder, a former researcher at the University of Kansas, Brené Brown says that hope happens when:

- We have the ability to set realistic goals (*I know where I want to go*).
- We are able to figure out how to achieve those goals, including the ability to stay flexible and develop alternative routes (*I know how to get there, I'm persistent, and I can tolerate disappointment and try again*).
- We believe in ourselves (*I can do this!*).[8]

So for all of us who are perpetually too hard on ourselves for not doing more or being more, let's set realistic goals, persevere through trials, and ask God for wisdom along the way (James 1:2–5). And let's believe that He will grant us that wisdom (James 1:6) and give us the strength we need (Philippians 4:13). "God is able to bless you abundantly, so that in all things at all times, having all that you need, you will abound in every good work" (2 Corinthians 9:8).

THE PITFALL OF PRIDE

Before my son's eighth birthday party began, I could tell my husband was not exactly in a festive mood. While I had spent the morning taking the kids to their drama classes, Rob had tackled projects we'd been putting off for months—things like replacing a gross toilet seat and gluing a broken dining room chair back together. He even ran out to buy a new, plastic Hot Wheels tablecloth after our cat had chewed holes in the first one. Oh, and, he'd also gotten up at three in the morning to work on a paper.

I pulled Rob aside. "Hey, I really appreciate you spending these last few hours getting things ready for the party," I told him. "I know you have a lot of grad school work to do and you're really tired. Thank you."

He nodded emphatically.

Happily, I caught myself before blurting out what instantly came to the tip of my tongue: *But I've been working on the details for weeks, sending invitations, shopping for supplies, buying gifts, wrapping gifts, planning the menu, baking the cake, and decorating, and—on top of all that—I'm behind on my book deadline!* I know, I know. Pride is so unbecoming.

Pride is the seedy underbelly of comparison. And let's just say it: for many of us, this can be a perpetual pitfall.

"This has long been my biggest issue!" confesses Roseanna White, an author friend of mine who also does graphic design. She explains:

Pride and I go way back—all the way back to primary school. This is a personality trait I've spent years getting under control. Step by step, I've learned how to identify those tendencies and nip them in the bud before they can lead to some major internal ugliness. But it's so easy to slip into.

Sometimes it'll sneak up to me on a blog I'm a guest on—comparing how many comments my post gets to someone else's. Or how many likes I get for something on Facebook. Or how many reviews my books have, or whether they're good. When I noticed that even good reviews were annoying me, I had to stop reading them altogether—it just wasn't healthy for me to do so.

For my part, I've had to come down to asking myself this: is this thing I'm doing something that's for me or for God? If it's for me, then it doesn't really matter. And if it's for God, then all that matters is that I'm pleasing Him—and when I'm living in pride, I know I'm not.

Whether comparisons result in envy or pride, the antidote is the same: to value others above ourselves (Philippians 2:3-4). Remember that, in Luke 10:18-20, Jesus reminded

His disciples that though they would be doing amazing things, they should not be in awe of themselves but of God's power to save. We, too, would do well to marvel more at the Lord's work than we do at anyone else's—including our own.

YOU ARE ENOUGH

If you listen carefully, you'll notice that messages pumped through much of our media tell us we are some version of "not enough." Not rich enough, not beautiful enough, not thin enough, not smart enough, not productive enough, not well-rested enough. Even if we don't buy the products that promise to make up for our lack, we often buy the *idea* that, compared to the rest of the world (or compared to who we could be), we are simply not enough.

My friend Kathy Collard Miller, author of the book *Never Ever Be the Same: A New You Starts Today*, co-authored with her husband, Larry, shared with me, "I compare myself to other mothers, wives, writers, and speakers. I think, 'Look at all they are doing and I'm not.' As a recovering perfectionist, if I wasn't doing it 'all,' I wasn't doing 'anything.' That's the all-or-nothing perspective of a perfectionist. But God has been dealing with this tendency for a long time because it essentially means I'm not trusting God."

Zechariah 4:10 showed Kathy a new perspective: "Who dares despise the day of small things, since the seven eyes of the LORD that range throughout the earth will rejoice when they see the chosen capstone in the hand of Zerubbabel?"

Kathy offers some context for this verse. "At the time of Zechariah's writing, some older people were unimpressed with the construction of the new Temple. They remembered the 'old' Temple that had been destroyed in their lifetime. They had seen the magnificent Temple built by Solomon, and to them, this replacement didn't compare. They called the new construction 'a small thing' but God (through Zechariah) says, 'Who is calling my work "small"? Anything I do is big!' That's his message through the prophet Haggai in Haggai 2:3-4, 9."

Those of us who feel that our offerings are "small" compared to the work of others can take great comfort from this refreshing perspective! Kathy offers these "small" thoughts to take to heart:

- "Small" doesn't mean "meaningless."
- What seems small is often the beginning of something big for God.
- God values "small" because He is glorified when it brings great results.
- God chooses weak vessels so that He will be glorified.
- Your first step is important—don't give up.
- Small steps add up.

Since publishing a book based on their triumph over his addiction to pornography, Jen and Craig Ferguson are building a marriage ministry together. During this process, she calls comparison a thorn in her side—but one she's grateful for, because it keeps her running to what she calls "the Jesus mirror."

"I'm super devoted to taking my thoughts captive right now, because as Craig and I participate in marriage ministry, it would be my method of operation to just focus on the building," Jen told me. "When I focus on the building, I get focused on the size. And then I see the size of other things. And it catapults from there. So I keep the Jesus mirror with me and turn to it when I feel tempted to do things just because of the twinge of envy or the crushing feelings of inadequacy. Jesus tells me I'm enough—even if I build nothing—because He built me."

And you, dear reader, are enough. Right now, today, you are enough. Cast aside differing weights and measures, abandon the false balance, and rest in the knowledge that you are complete in Christ. You are whole. You are already enough because of God's work for you, in you, and through you.

Her Greatest Reward

It should have been one of the proudest moments of Shawn Johnson's life. But as the sixteen-year-old gymnast from Iowa stood on the podium at the Beijing Olympic Games, the person who draped the silver medal around her neck hugged her and whispered, "I'm sorry."[9]

Shawn had just given the best routine of her life, but it wasn't enough to win gold. Hearing "I'm sorry," she said, "was kind of like a validation in my heart that I had failed. I got two more silver after that and then finally got a gold but once I got the gold, it didn't matter. I felt like the damage was done."

Prior to the Games, sports news outlets had predicted Shawn would take home four gold medals, and because she didn't, "I felt like I had failed the world. I felt like since the world saw me as nothing else, then if I failed at being a gymnast, I failed at being a human being."

After the Olympics, Shawn went on to become the youngest contestant in the history of *Dancing with the Stars*. "I was sixteen years old, a muscular gymnast and I was not even 4'8". And I was dancing next to girls who were supermodels. . . . People criticized my weight and my appearance and my personality and my character. It affected me immensely. It drove me to try to change everything about myself. Trying to act like someone you aren't and trying to look like someone you will never be is exhausting and draining."

Shawn won that competition, by the way. But comparisons had stolen her joy.

Assuming the answer was a gymnastic comeback, she trained for the 2012 Olympic Games. About six months before the Olympic trials, however, she hit her all-time low. She was spending more than forty hours a week training, constantly trying to lose weight, but it wasn't happening.

"I was losing hair, I wasn't able to sleep, I wasn't eating properly," Shawn remembers. "For months, I just pushed myself in practice." Every day, she'd come home "just bawling and bawling and not having any outlet of peace."

Then one day, everything changed as she stood at the edge of the balance beam in practice, preparing to start flipping. "In that one moment, I felt like God was telling me,

'You've been so distraught over this decision and you've been putting yourself through all this, and your family through all this, and you've been afraid of disappointing a lot of people and you've not been yourself. But it's okay to follow your heart and to put it behind you.' In that instant, I felt the entire world lifted off my shoulders. In that one instant, I knew it was all going to be okay.

"I was giving my heart and soul and getting to a place that I was not proud of, all for that gold medal again, even though I distinctly remember in 2008 not being the greatest thing in the world. . . . God is the answer to everything. Jesus sacrificed his life on the cross so that when I stood up there and I was given that gold medal, yes it's a monumental and amazing experience and a wonderful thing, but it's not the end all be all. Yes, I can work my whole life to be the CEO of a company or to make a certain amount of money, or to win twelve more Olympic gold medals, but it's not the purpose in life. He will always be my greatest reward and my proudest reward."

Your Turn

1. To whom do you most often compare yourself? Why?
2. When are you most vulnerable to making comparisons?
3. Who is it that you most want to please?
4. Which false standards can you release?
5. How can you adjust your expectations of yourself to be more realistic for your current season?

Truths to Trust

Comparison steals joy.
You are already enough, and complete in Christ.

Romans 12:1-6

CHAPTER 4

What are we free from — Free
from Wordly advice — Free to stop

Voices and and listen
Choices

"The gatekeeper opens the gate for him, and the sheep listen to
his voice. He calls his own sheep by name and leads them out."

JOHN 10:3

God's voice resonates within us because it speaks in
a language that we, by the power of the Holy Spirit,
can completely comprehend.

PRISCILLA SHIRER
Discerning the Voice of God: How to Recognize When God Speaks

Stop and Listen

My stomach was in knots. But this was why I'd come to this large conference for Christian fiction writers: for these fifteen-minute appointments during which I could pitch my next book to top editors in the industry. My previous publisher was no longer acquiring novels, so it was time to find another one.

I'd say it took all of thirty seconds for me to strike out with the first editor. (But wait, there's more.) After telling me that I was "young, just *so* young," (I was thirty-eight), and that it was next to impossible to break into Christian fiction these days (which I had already done), this woman gave me some advice: Give up, she said. Forget writing for the inspirational market, there's too much competition, too many authors who have been doing this forever, authors like Karen Kingsbury. Who can compete with her? Go secular, write romance, that's where the money is anyway.

"Mainstream romance?" I asked with a jolt. I don't even write Christian romance.

"Add some sex, if you have the chops," she advised. Then she told me to go read the works of several romance novelists whose book covers make me blush. "You'll have to do that, of course."

(I did mention that this took place at a *Christian* conference, for writers of faith-based fiction, right?)

But she wasn't done yet. "You want to be the CEO of your own business, don't you?" Fired up by her own speech, she began punching the air for emphasis. "You want to get that next contract that will give you enough money to keep writing, so you can get the next contract, and the next. That's what it's all about—go where the money is and you might have a long career."

I'm not sure how long I sat there, too stunned to re-spond, but it was long enough for the woman to ask if I was okay.

I wasn't.

"It's your choice," she said, and shrugged.

On that point, at least, we agreed.

THE PARADOX OF CHOICE

Choices can be a double-edged sword. They promise free-dom, but they also allow for relentless second-guessing. I chose not to follow that editor's advice of writing smutty novels to make a living. But since the counsel came from someone deemed "successful" in the Christian publishing industry, our little tête-à-tête did cause me to question my ability to find a publisher for what I felt called to write.

Doubt trailed me for the rest of that conference. Maybe she was right—there's no hope for me to get another Christian novel published. Maybe I shouldn't have taken that nine-month sabbatical to recover from seven years of nonstop deadlines. Maybe I'll never get another novel pub-lished again. That's it. I'm done. These were not comforting thoughts, but they were ultimately false. The book I pitched to this editor, *The Mark of the King*, did find a wonderful home with a Christian publishing house. Smut-free and all.

In the first chapter of this book, we looked at a study which found that women in America are unhappier than ever. We explored a possible reason: the lack of purpose cou-pled with the pressure to excel in multiple domains. But there may be another cause for our unhappiness, according to the authors of that report: it's something psychologist and Swarthmore College professor Barry Schwartz calls "the paradox of choice."

Schwartz explains it this way: Western industrial societies like to maximize the welfare of citizens by maximizing their freedom, and "the way to maximize freedom is to maximize choice."[1] Take a stroll through the typical grocery store and count the number of cereals offered. Step inside Best Buy and try not to be overwhelmed by the options in phones and cameras. Prescription drugs are marketed to us as consumers, even though it's the doctors who prescribe—and it's all because our culture is obsessed with choices.

But Schwartz points out some unforeseen negatives this plethora of choice has on people. "One effect, paradoxically, is that it produces paralysis, rather than liberation. With so many options to choose from, people find it very difficult to choose at all," he says. "The second effect is that even if we manage to overcome the paralysis and make a choice, we end up less satisfied with the result of the choice than we would be if we had fewer options to choose from. . . . The more options there are, the easier it is to regret anything at all that is disappointing about the option that you chose." The concept applies both to the products we buy and the choices we make in our daily lives.

The interesting thing about the study on declining female happiness is that the downward trend is consistent across many areas of life, irrespective of marital or employment status or whether the women have young children. Haven't we all experienced that in our own lives? Think about it: when we see another woman who seems to be happier with her decisions than we are with ours, it's easy to wonder if we've chosen the wrong path. But certainly it's not just the choices we make (and don't make) that can cause dissatisfaction. It's the voices that come along with them.

Two of my best friends from college live in the same Midwestern city, and both of them have experienced this, though their lives look very different from each other. When Annabel, a social worker and pastor's wife, announced that she planned to stay home full time once her baby was born, "Someone without kids asked me, 'How long do you expect this season of your life to last?' I was so caught off guard. How was I to know how long it was going to last? That was up to God! But it made me feel like I was going off the grid or something. It made me feel like it wasn't valued."

Meanwhile, our friend Charlotte is a doctor while raising two children with her husband, who is also a doctor. "I've had other moms in my neighborhood ask me if I 'have to work'—like the only reason they think a mom would work is because the husband did not make enough money," she told me. "I tell them I choose to work, and they usually change the subject. I just know that I have a meaningful job as a doctor that gives a lot of purpose to my life. I still have bad days but I really do think I am doing what God wants me to be doing—and that allows me to feel good about my decisions."

Many times the voices that are the most difficult to respond to come from those closest to us. "My mother frequently marvels at how my husband does extra at home and with the kids in order to support me in my achieving my dreams," my friend Teresa told me. "Though I agree with the sentiment, I also feel a bit of a sting. She doesn't mean to be negative, but I can't help hearing, 'You're not doing everything you should.' How can I respond? Mom's right—my husband does do a lot. I try very hard to take these words in the way she meant them, and to remember to be thankful for the support that I have. I also remind her that seeing me work hard and persevere is a good thing for my children. And spending time with Dad is a good thing for them, too!"

I've known my friend Krista since we were both working in Washington, DC. Then, she was the senior legislative aide to a congresswoman. Today, she's vice president for strategy and innovation at her company, and she says the inner voice is the loudest. She is also a pastor's wife, and she's giving herself permission not to lead as many ministries as she did before she had her three children so she can spend more time with the kids. "I still put pressure on myself," she told me. "I miss a lot of church committee meetings, and though I haven't been made to feel bad about that, sometimes I still do. The voice in my own head is far louder than any real person."

All of us hear criticisms, whether blatant or subtle, from strangers, family, or even ourselves. It's how we respond that matters.

RESONANCE

Of course, not every voice we hear should be dismissed. "Plans fail for lack of counsel, but with many advisers they succeed" (Proverbs 15:22). "A word fitly spoken is like apples of gold in a setting of silver" (Proverbs 25:11 ESV). The first part of this verse in the New Living Translation says, "Timely advice is lovely." So how do we untangle the words worth listening to from those that aren't?

Music provides a clue. I once attended a Bible conference where this was demonstrated onstage. A woman opened the lid of the grand piano, exposing the strings and hammers beneath it. Then she sang a single, clear note while holding a microphone close to the strings inside the instrument. When her voice faded away, we could all hear that a string was still vibrating in response to her note. She sang a C, and the string for that key on the piano hummed in agreement with her, though no one had touched that C key on the piano. I'd been playing the piano for many years by that point, but I was amazed by the illustration. That's resonance.

The Holy Spirit works the same way with us. When we are in tune with Him—by spending consistent time in the Word and in prayer—something that resonates with us can probably be trusted. But if something doesn't resonate with what we know to be true, we know it's not in line with what God wants for us.

There's no shortage of advice, is there? People bombard us in a steady stream—over social media and the Internet, television, radio, even in person, whether friends or strangers. As an author, I hear from sweet readers who probably think too highly of me, and from strangers who attack my character because they disagree with something I've written. Some people we invite to speak into our lives: the editor I met at that conference is just one example. Pastors, family members, and friends are others.

In times past, when people suggested to Jen Ferguson that she'd overcommitted herself, she was defensive. "I argued back with all the 'good' I was doing," she told me. "Now, I've learned that I easily overdo, and I have to let people tell me when I'm getting crazy. I started asking my husband to be my 'crazy barometer.' I try not to argue when he reflects me back to me. I just have to go grab my Jesus mirror, which tells me I'm enough even without all my striving."

IT'S A SIGN! (OR IS IT?)

The day Madeleine L'Engle turned forty, she opened a rejection letter from a publisher, deemed it "an obvious sign from heaven," and gave up writing. Sobbing, she covered the typewriter in her study and paced the room. "The rejection on my fortieth birthday seemed an unmistakable command: Stop this foolishness and learn to make cherry pie," she wrote.

But even as she wept, her mind was hatching a novel about failure. Could she have misinterpreted the "obvious sign" and the "unmistakable command"?

"I uncovered the typewriter," she later wrote of that day. "In my journal I recorded this moment of decision, for that's what it was. I had to write. It was not up to me to say I would stop, because I could not. . . . If I never had another book published, and it was very clear to me that this was a real possibility, I still had to go on writing."[2]

After four years and more than two dozen rejections, *A Wrinkle in Time* was finally published. It won the Newbery Medal in 1963, and Madeleine went on to publish more than sixty books over the course of her life.

I love this story for the tenacity it represents. But at the same time, I shudder at the thought of Madeleine calling it quits on writing because she originally mistook her birthday rejection as a sign. Thankfully, we don't have to base our life decisions on external signs and voices alone.

EAR TRAINING

When it comes to seeking guidance for the future—even for the right now—the Holy Spirit is so much more reliable than "signs." But it also takes a practiced ear to listen for Him. We need to train ourselves to hear Him above everything else.

Jesus, who sent the Holy Spirit to live inside believers after He had ascended to heaven, once said, "I am the good shepherd; I know my sheep and my sheep know me—just as the Father knows me and I know the Father—and I lay down my life for the sheep. I have other sheep that are not of this sheep pen. I must bring them also. They too will listen to my voice, and there shall be one flock and one shepherd" (John 10:14–16).

We need to listen for the voice of Christ, through His Holy Spirit, in our lives. As we've already discussed, God can use people to speak truth into our circumstances—but we need to be discerning as we sort through all the advice we receive.

Thankfully, our Good Shepherd will never steer us wrong. In John 10:14, Jesus says He and His sheep know each other. People who don't know me at all have offered the worst advice I've received in life. But even those closest to us can suggest things that do not align with God's leading for us.

So how can we hear what He's saying? How do we know a word is from Him?

Reading God's Word will help us discern whether the leading we sense is consistent with the whole character of God. And, of course, we pray. But—here's the toughest part—we also have to *listen*, which usually means allowing time before making decisions. The more we read, pray, and listen, the easier it will become to recognize His voice and understand how He wants us to order not only our lives, but our days.

I first met author Julie Lessman in an online book club forum after I'd read some of her novels. Since then, she's become one of a host of kindred spirit friends, though miles separate us. "I have always prayed about everything I do, but I've realized in the last few years that although my lips lined up with wanting God's will, my own will often directed my actions, which often got me in over my head as a writer," she told me. What she did next may have made her editors and agent nervous, but it made all the difference in her life:

> I took an eight-month sabbatical to focus more on God, family, and writing for the sheer joy of writing, and it was the best thing I've ever done. Over that time I wrote my most important and spiritual book to date, *Isle of Hope*. Make no mistake—I have always loved God and sought to please Him. But it wasn't until this sabbatical that I finally realized I had given my heart and allegiance to other things as well, robbing Him of the glory due only to Him. Through this period of seeking God like never before, I fully understood—both in my heart and in mind—that He is everything in life. . . . I now decide how to spend my energy through a far deeper relationship with the Holy Spirit than ever before, truly seeking God's will for my career rather than my own.

Julie reaped a harvest of peace and purpose from the time and space she dedicated to really listening to God. Likewise, once we sense a leading from the Lord, "Expect the mercy of confirmation," writes Priscilla Shirer in *Discerning the Voice of God*. "Look for God's use of circumstances, Scripture, and other believers to confirm His direction for your life."[3]

It's important to note here that God does use circumstances to guide us, but they work in tandem with the Bible, the promptings of the Holy Spirit, and biblical counsel. Opposition, for example, does not always mean a "closed door." Jesus himself faced plenty of opposition on this earth. The apostle Paul was shipwrecked, stoned, lashed, and imprisoned, but never mistook those circumstances as "signs" that his work should stop. Let's not allow the cultural preference for "fun, fast, and easy" to trick us into believing that what is difficult is not worth the time and effort required.

I love Roseanna White's perspective on seeking guidance for how to spend her time. She told me, "Mostly, I just pray that the Lord ignites that passion in me for the work He wants me to do. *Passion*, at its root, involves suffering. So a good question to ask is, 'Am I willing to suffer for this? To sacrifice for it?' The answer isn't often *yes*. Most things are just passing phases for us. But then that thing will come along that we *are* willing to sacrifice for. And that's when I know it's what God wants me to focus on."

Estimating the Cost (Luke 14:28)

Asking yourself the following questions may help you estimate the cost of accepting a new responsibility or role:

- Does this line up with my big-picture purpose?
- Am I passionate about this?
- How would accepting this commitment affect my capacity to serve and love those closest to me?
- Am I qualified for and capable of meeting this need?
- Will I be operating within my strengths, or will this commitment be draining?
- How much time (including preparation) will this require, and how long will the commitment last?
- How will this impact my schedule in my current season? Do I have the time it would take to give this the attention it deserves?
- What would I have to decline if I say yes to this opportunity? Is this an acceptable trade-off?
- Am I motivated to answer a certain way out of fear, guilt, or obligation?
- How would saying yes affect my family? How do they feel about it?
- Do I have the financial resources to comfortably say yes?
- Do I have the emotional energy required for this commitment?
- What does my gut say?
- What do I sense God telling me about this?

BEWARE THE "YES MIRROR"

Experiencing opposition and criticism doesn't always mean you're making the wrong choice. But receiving praise and flattery doesn't guarantee we're on the right track, either.

We all need backup singers, those who not only believe in us but lift us up, even singing for us when we forget our own music. We need friends who sing truth to us until we can sing it ourselves—they support us, harmonize with us, and help us make sense of life together. And they do this not from a distance, but from the same stage—or in the same mess—as ourselves. We need them.

What we don't need, however, are the voices that tell us "yes" no matter what.

In my college dorm room I had a full-length mirror that everyone loved. Girls would traipse into my room just to admire their reflections, especially before going out on dates. Each person's image, slightly distorted to appear leaner than the reality, was an irresistible confidence booster. I called it the "Yes Mirror" because those who saw themselves exclaimed, "Yes!"

The problem with that mirror was that I forgot *why* it was so popular, and I began to trust my reflection. Had I weighed myself regularly, I would have noticed a growing problem (pun intended). But even as my waistband tightened, Yes Mirror still told me what I wanted to hear. "You look good, girl! Twizzlers at midnight? *Yes!* After all, you're up studying. You deserve a treat!"

Then I went home for the summer, to the land of regular, truth-telling mirrors. Oh, the revelation. Yes Mirror had done me no favors, and I had to live with the proof.

Be careful who you listen to. Keep your backup singers, those rare and precious friends who truly support you. But beware of those who would urge you to say yes to commitments you normally wouldn't make.

My friend Dana was involved with a wonderful Bible study for seven years. "They asked me for two years to be a leader and I kept saying no because I knew the time commitment would be a stress on my family," she told me. "The leaders of the group were wonderful, but they kept urging me, saying that I would be a great leader. On the third year, I relented and, with my husband's permission, said yes."

After a couple years, Dana knew it was time to step down. But the group leaders kept asking her to serve again, and in a "weak moment," she relented. Partway into the commitment, however, God opened the door to a part-time job like Dana had been seeking for some time. "The last few months of the Bible study were really hard, and I was so stressed out," she said. "I barely finished my lessons, getting to meetings was hard, and I had to rearrange my work schedule. It's hard to say no to something so good like leading a Bible study—but in the end I wasn't able to give the study and my group the energy they deserved. It's an act of faith to say no and believe that God will bring someone else along, that He is in charge and His work will get done . . . without me."

After several people asked Jen Ferguson to participate in a Jog-a-thon at her children's school, she said yes. "I thought, *I'm a runner. I have kids. I want kids to be healthy. I want our school to raise money. I should do this.* And I fit in the meetings and signed up to get sponsorships—and the day of the event, I missed out on all the fun because I was sick. I had run myself totally ragged. God had told me it wasn't my season to volunteer at the school, but I thought I knew better than God."

I can't think of a single thing people have asked me to do that wasn't a "good" thing. I'll bet you can say the same. But to fully lean into our God-given purposes, we can't settle for good. We must choose the *best* fit for what we're called to do and be.

GOOD VERSUS BEST

On the daily level, the choices filling our time are literally endless. As a glutton for guilt (now recovering), I have had a hard time saying no to many requests.

My garden again provides example. I had read that one of my spring chores should be to strip off the smallest peony buds, leaving only the largest one to grow on each stalk. That way, the plant would put all of its energy into one bloom per stalk. Rather than having several small flowers, I could look forward to "show-stopping blooms" instead.

I immediately marched outside and set to work pinching off the smaller buds. Each time I dropped one to the mulch below, I pondered the similarities to the way I must manage my time when I'm trying to grow something beautiful—usually a book, always my children. I have to say no to several small, good things, so I can pour my energy into something bigger and better

But pinching peonies is one thing. Responding to a fellow human being is quite another.

The day after I "learned" this lesson, someone asked me to do a good thing that needed to be done. I cringed when I read the request in my in-box. This person was asking for time that I had already set aside for writing. I had already arranged childcare.

"Pinch the peony!" I told myself. "Tell her you can't do it! You're already committed!" Still, I struggled. I prayed, deliberated, prayed some more, and finally asked a trusted friend to weigh in. Being the wise woman she is, my friend affirmed my gut reaction. I had to pinch the peony to preserve my energy for the best thing.

We are allowed to discern where our service will do the most good, given our skills, gifts, and experience. Otherwise, writes Lysa TerKeurst, "We become slaves to others' demands when we let our time become dictated by requests. We will live reactive lives instead of proactive. And reactive lives get very exhausting, very quickly. . . . This isn't just about finding time. This is about honoring God with the time we have."[4]

But maybe you can relate to how one woman responded to this concept. Beth, who I met through a mutual friend, told me, "I wish I were that thoughtful and deliberate. More often than not I'm making decisions on the fly and spending energy on whatever is 'next.' My spiritual life and my physical health suffer as a result."

If you feel the same way, reflect on your current pattern of decision making and what you'd like that to be from this point forward. Don't allow guilt to get in the way. It's never too late—or too early—to begin making thoughtful, strategic choices.

We all need time for what God has called us to do in our particular season. That doesn't mean we should say no to *every* request that comes our way—in fact, sometimes after considering an opportunity I'm convinced I'll decline, God will surprise me by leading me to accept it. Other times, I've turned down projects that lined up with my big-picture purpose because I knew it would pull too much of me away from my family. The more we tune our ears to God's leading, the clearer the right choice will become.

"I have this fear of white spaces on my calendar," Shannon Popkin admits. "I'm not sure how to face them, so I agree to help and serve and give. And while there's nothing wrong with setting my default to 'yes' when considering opportunities to serve God, I need to spend more time asking God to direct my paths."

Shannon points to Isaiah 30:1-2 (ESV), which says, "'Ah, stubborn children,' declares the LORD, 'who carry out a plan, but not mine . . . who set out to go down to Egypt without asking for my direction.'" These verses show that God wants to lead and direct us, says Shannon, who expounds on this concept in her excellent book, *Control Girl: Lessons on Surrendering Your Burden of Control from Seven Women in the Bible*. "He loves it when we ask for direction."

One year, after agreeing to lead a weekly Bible study, which also required her participation in a separate weekly coaching session for leaders, Shannon worried it would prove to be too much. "But as I prayed about what to do, I sensed God stirring me to continue being involved. I prayed for a way to limit my commitment to one morning per week." In a surprising answer to prayer, Shannon's women's ministry leader asked if she would consider being a coach to other leaders—on Monday mornings only. "I'll get to coach and disciple the leaders of the young moms groups," she told

17

Psalm 139:18

me. "I can't think of a better fit, for both my calendar and my God-given gifts and passions!"

Shannon's still learning how to navigate the fine line between overcommitting and serving as heartily as she can. "But one thing I know," she says, "God loves to guide my steps. If my service is for Him, I need to let Him decide how best to use me."

Listen for God's leading, and make your best choices yet.

A Voice for Authenticity

From 1998 to 2002, singer and songwriter Nichole Nordeman produced three albums that were popular both with fans and critics, and in 2003 collected four Dove Awards. In 2005, she released another critically acclaimed album, titled *Brave*—and then she proved how brave she really was.

She stopped.

At a time of her greatest professional momentum, when so many voices clamored for more of hers, she quietly went home to focus on her family.

"I had been working for many, many years to build up to that point," Nichole said. "I was selling records pretty well, touring a lot, and really experiencing blessing and favor. I felt at that time like I was really struggling with balance in my personal life, and I had been for some time. My marriage was in trouble. I was a new mom. I know so many artists and friends of mine who are able to make

Jeremiah 33:3

those two worlds live together in tandem. They bring nannies on the road and they homeschool on the tour bus. That just never felt like a fit for me, and so I was subsequently not being a great artist or a great mom."[5]

Nichole's fans didn't want her to stop writing songs, singing, recording, or touring. A part of her own heart struggled with the choice, too. But it was God's voice that guided her.

"I really felt like God said, 'This is not even something I'm asking you to slow down. I'm asking you to stop,' just to hit the brakes, which was a really hard decision at that particular time in my career," she said. "It was very difficult just to say to all these people who'd been working so hard with me and for me that I'm going to take that hat off completely. I did that for almost a decade to stay home with my babies."[6]

During that time, she wrote a book and seventeen songs for a project called *The Story*. She just didn't need to leave home to do it. When *Christianity Today* asked why Nichole wasn't touring with the artists who were singing the songs she'd written, she replied: "As much as I would love to take the stage with these phenomenal artists, I still feel the tug to be home right now. . . . I feel like I'll know when and if God gives me the green light to go back on the road. And it's just not now."[7]

Nichole's 2015 album, *The Unmaking*, is named for the song which acknowledges the heartache she'd experienced since her previous release. "I'm sad to say that my marriage did not survive, and that's been part of the unmaking that God's been working in my life. He's been so kind to me in helping me understand that crisis and disaster and personal failure and sorrow do not have to be something to be ashamed of or be hidden. . . . Truly I felt like God said to me over the past ten years of a very broken marriage and nine and a half years of trying to resuscitate it every day, 'It's okay to sit in this rubble a little bit. Let's not pretend because you are Nichole Nordeman that all is well if it's not well because there is strength.' His strength is in our weakness. He's very clear about that. The song is about that."[8]

In a culture and an industry where the pressure to push forward can be crushing, Nichole Nordeman listened to God's prompting over everyone else's and found her strength in Him.

Your Turn

1. Whose voices are you most listening to right now?
2. How can you tune in more clearly to God's voice?
3. When was the last time someone gave you advice that didn't resonate with you? What did you do?
4. Which questions from the "Estimating the Cost" sidebar will you especially keep in mind the next time you need to make a decision?
5. What are some good things you may need to release to make room for the best things?

Truths to Trust

God's voice is more important—but not always louder—than everyone else's. Choosing the best over the good is wise stewardship.

CHAPTER 5

Stay in agreement

Seizing God

*It is the LORD your God you must follow, and him you must revere.
Keep his commands and obey him; serve him and hold fast to him.*

DEUTERONOMY 13:4

*When I grow up, I mean way, way up, I hope to be a wise
old woman of God. Someone who has learned not merely to
seize the day, but to seize the Lord.*

CAROLYN WEBER
Holy Is the Day: Living in the Gift of the Present

Speak it!

May I confess something to you? When I woke up yesterday, I was not ready for another day. I was aware of my husband rolling out of bed a little after four o'clock, and I was aware that if I wanted a jump start on my workday, I should do the same.

The fact that I feel like a slacker for sleeping in until five should tell you something about our current season. We are both running as hard as we can. We both see the light at the end of the tunnel—for him, it's the semester's end, and for me, it's four months from now, after I've finished two book manuscripts. Really, four months is not that far off on the calendar—but right now, I'm so sick of running. Which is ironic, granted, because this entire book is built on the premise that there is freedom in leaning in to our purpose. We are free to run the race set out for us, as the apostle Paul wrote to the Corinthians.

Well friends, I'm leaning in. As I write this, I'm launching four books—two fiction, two nonfiction—in the next eleven months. It will probably prove to be the most tightly-packed release schedule of my writing life. Weekly, daily, I'm adjusting and recalculating what I should and shouldn't do. And I don't feel one bit guilty about it—I feel a deep sense of purpose and the abiding joy that comes with that.

But, man, I'm tired. Not the two-cups-of-coffee kind of tired. The kind of tired where I stand in the predawn shadows of my kitchen and stare at the microwave clock in a stupor. My husband prays for me to have a productive day, and my heart whimpers, "No God, please no, that does not sound good to me today." The kind of tired when I start an email message to myself as a reminder—and I suddenly have no idea, none whatsoever, what it was I was trying not to forget. That kind of tired.

I'm uncomfortable admitting that I struggle with burn-out or weariness because I don't want to seem ungrateful for the things which require my time. Somewhere along the way, I must have bought into the idea that stress and blessings are mutually exclusive—the phrase "too blessed to be stressed" rattles around in my head. I don't know who said it first, but what once sounded like a harmlessly cheerful thought now just adds a layer of shame that I am, in fact, both blessed and stressed.

In the movie *Dead Poets Society*, the unconventional teacher (played by Robin Williams) takes his students to a trophy case and tells them to peer through the glass at photos of athletes who are now in their graves. In a creepy and compelling whisper, Williams pretends to be the voice of the dead. "*Carpe diem*," he says. "Seize the day, boys. Make your lives extraordinary."

I've always been inspired by that scene. But right now, I don't have it in me to *carpe* one more *diem*.

You know where I'm coming from, don't you? Doing the right thing—living on purpose, answering the daily call of Christlike service—can be tiring even on good days. Then my thoughts veer toward friends and readers whose days may not seem good at all right now:

- those who have children with special needs, who spend hours every week fighting insurance companies, visiting doctors and therapists, or just trying to feed their kids—and cleaning up vomit when their little bodies reject food.
- those who are the constant caregivers for husbands whose war injuries may or may not be

visible to society, but that render them incapable of functioning the way they used to.

- those who suffer chronic pain and complex medical challenges which can make daily life seem like a hike up Mount Everest.

Suddenly, *carpe diem* sounds like crazy talk. Some days all we can ask for is to get through the day, let alone seize it.

In *Holy Is the Day: Living in the Gift of the Present*, Carolyn Weber offers a profound and refreshing perspective on what *carpe diem* should look like in the believer's everyday life. "Perhaps the answer lies in when *carpe diem* evokes worship, when it is a form of honoring the God who is honoring us with his presence. Put another way, when *carpe diem* becomes *carpe Deum*, or, translated loosely for our purposes here, 'Seize God!'"[1]

Can you hear me sighing with relief right now? Seize God! Hold onto Him, as Deuteronomy 13:4 says. That's something I can do. The Bible is full of stories of others who have seized Him, too.

SEIZE GOD'S BLESSING

In Genesis 32, Jacob was afraid for his life. Years earlier, he had fled from his brother, Esau, who was in a murderous rage over being tricked out of his birthright for a bowl of soup. Now, after God had already promised that he would prosper, Jacob had wives, children, servants, and livestock aplenty—and he heard that Esau was coming to meet him. Jacob feared that his brother was coming to kill not only him, but his wives and children as well. To soften Esau, Jacob sent servants bearing gifts before they met.

That night, Jacob literally wrestled with God, demanding a blessing (Genesis 32:22–32). God granted it and renamed him Israel, "because you have struggled with God and with humans and have overcome" (verse 28). The Ryrie Study Bible footnote for this verse says the name *Israel* means "he fights or persists with God (in prevailing prayer)." Other Bible footnotes define the name as "struggles with God" or "strives against God."

Let's think about this for a moment. God blessed Israel because of his struggling, striving, persisting, prevailing prayer. Elijah, Moses, Abraham, and David grappled fiercely as well. Not only are we allowed to be bold in our prayers, but God *wants* us to be. When we struggle with an issue, we are to take that struggle to God—even if it means fighting with Him.

Only when we let ourselves fight with God do "we find ourselves close enough to hear Him . . . [which] places us close enough that, when we're spent and collapse into depression, we fall into the only arms that can really console us in our grief and loss," writes Laurie Wallin, mother of four children, two of whom have multiple mental health issues.[2] Don't be afraid to let God hear exactly how you feel and what you think. He can take it!

For Rebekah Benimoff, the blessing is God himself. She says:

A precious Presence in my life, this Voice leads, guides, calms me when medical chaos—or life in general—would otherwise overwhelm me. It's when I get to a quiet place and be still that I recognize He *is* the blessing—whether I am "happy" or not, whether life is what I want or not, whether a storm is raging or not.

There is only One who *is* the gift in my every moment. I am at peace in God alone. Happy? Not recently, no. But joy comes as I connect to the One who is my Source—the One who moves me to greater wellness whether it's enjoyable or not.

I used to want to be happy—and while I don't object to happiness (I still prefer it to those other emotions) at the end of the day I have to confess I'd rather be whole.

SEIZE GOD'S PRESENCE

Jesus's visit to the home of Mary and Martha is probably a familiar story. If you're like me, you harbor a certain sympathy for Martha, who just wants to get the job done. I'm a task-oriented person, too, and where would we be without people like us? Then I recognize that my defensiveness is like a "check engine" light coming on. The trouble I mentioned at the beginning of this chapter—my exhaustion with the whole *carpe diem* thing—is an indication that I really need to read this story in Luke 10:38–42 again. For the seven thousandth time.

It still convicts me. Martha was "distracted" by her tasks, which means the main priority was something else—fellowship with Jesus. So I have to ask myself: Do I have things backwards? Do I view my to-do list as the main priority, and fellowship as the distraction? In sitting at the feet of Jesus, Mary had "chosen what is better, and it will not be taken away from her." Time spent with God, in His presence, has eternal value.

In John 12, we get another look at these same sisters. As their brother, Lazarus, reclined at the table with Jesus, Martha was serving again (bless her!). And Mary once again knelt at Jesus's feet, this time anointing them with perfume and wiping them with her hair. When she was criticized for being wasteful by Judas Iscariot (not such a shining example of character himself, as it turned out), Jesus rebuked him.

In this passage, Mary was once again seizing Jesus, this time literally, as she lavishly expressed her love and reverence for Him. I have a lot to learn from Mary, but I see something else here which I hadn't noticed before: Martha is in the scene, too, serving. She's working to bring a meal to those at the table, but this time, she isn't reprimanded for being "distracted." Jesus doesn't point out that she's worried and upset about many things—likely because she isn't. She's doing the work, but she's still in the presence of the Lord.

I take great comfort in this, because as much as I enjoy my quiet time in the morning, I can't stay there all day. I have my children to teach and care for, meals to prepare, clothes to wash, words to write. You and I have things to do. But instead of choosing work *over* the presence of God, we can remain in God's presence *while* we work.

Too often, we compartmentalize our faith by relegating "spiritual thoughts" to the quiet time or to Sunday mornings. But we can seize the presence of God no matter the time of day or night.

He is present in our human moments. He is present here today, as I write at my parents' house while my husband watches the kids at ours. I get to use my mother's Bible, and I'm struck by all the notes in the margins. For years, even though her Bible was falling apart, she refused to get a new one because of all the sermon notes she'd added to the pages. So my dad bought her a new Bible and transcribed every single note to it, and she's been adding to those ever since. I see the handwriting of both parents in the margins of this Bible, and I take a moment to be in awe of the legacy of faith they have given me. I feel God's presence with every crackling turn of the page as I see how His Word has touched my family.

God was present yesterday, too, when I hit a writing wall and set work aside for my family's Annual Applesauce-Making Day. I sense Him now, showing me that my taking a break was His gift to me, that enjoying my family and His provision through the harvest was a way to *carpe Deum* on the day I really did not want to *carpe diem* anyway. I sensed Him when I confessed on my Facebook author page that I needed prayer to see me through my deadline, and encouragement and prayers came pouring in. Honestly, it felt like anointing. In all of this, I feel the Lord.

SEIZE GOD'S HEALING

I love the story in Mark 5:25–34 about the woman who had been bleeding for twelve years and had spent all she had on doctors and cures . . . in vain. "When she heard about Jesus, she came up behind him in the crowd and touched his cloak, because she thought, 'If I just touch his clothes, I will be healed.' Immediately her bleeding stopped and she felt in her body that she was freed from her suffering" (vv. 27–29).

The woman's bleeding had made her ceremonially un-clean and chronically anemic, but it probably wasn't obvious to others in the crowd that she was suffering. Jesus's instant healings of lepers, the blind, and the demon-possessed were far more dramatic, but a couple of things are worth noting here. First, she seized Jesus, if only by the hem of His garment. After twelve years without cure, she sought Him out, she reached for Him and she grabbed on to hope.

Second, we get to read what this woman told herself: "If I just touch his clothes, I will be healed." What we tell ourselves matters. And sometimes, we have to talk ourselves into seizing God.

One pitch-black morning in Alaska, when my husband was at sea and I was living alone among strangers, I feared the effects of the darkness and isolation on me. "It's happening again," I told myself. Years earlier, I'd been diagnosed with clinical depression. And though God had healed me from that, I felt vulnerable to someday sinking back into despair. But by predicting it, I was in danger of creating a self-fulfilling prophecy.

Those with serious depression find that willpower alone is not enough to bring healing. I'm so grateful for the doctors that God used to help bring me out of my darkest days. In this case in Alaska, however, I was able to stop my emotional slide when I told myself, "It's just a bad day. Everyone has them. I'm allowed to have bad days and good days." No longer did I feel doomed to repeat the past. I felt like a normal military wife with normal ups and downs.

What we tell ourselves matters. Proverbs 23:7 says, "For as he thinks within himself, so he is" (NASB). It's critical that what we tell ourselves matches God's truth. When we're tempted to tell ourselves, "I can't do this," we can align it with the truth by saying instead, "I can do all this through him who gives me strength" (Philippians 4:13). That's the lesson I appreciate most from the story of the woman in Mark 5.

It's a lesson that was powerfully demonstrated by Corrie ten Boom, after she survived the Nazi concentration camp that claimed the life of her dear sister. In 1947, in a church in Munich, Germany, she shared her story of being imprisoned during World War II for hiding Jews in her Haarlem, Holland, home. She spoke of her experience as an inmate under dreadful conditions, of the loss of her family members during the war, of God's forgiveness of sins, and of the need for people also to forgive those who had wronged them.

At the end of the service, a man approached Corrie. She recognized him as one of the guards at Ravensbrück. He'd been among the most vicious, and had mocked the women prisoners as they showered. "It came back with a rush," she wrote, "the huge room with its harsh overhead lights; the pathetic pile of dresses and shoes in the center of the floor; the shame of walking naked past this man."

Now here he was, in the same church with Corrie, hand outstretched to shake hers, saying:

> "A fine message, Fraulein! How good it is to know that, as you say, all our sins are at the bottom of the sea!"

> And I, who had spoken so glibly of forgiveness, fumbled in my pocketbook rather than take that hand. He would not remember me, of course—how could he remember one prisoner among those thousands of women?

The Hiding Place

But I remembered him and the leather crop swinging from his belt. I was face to face with one of my captors, and my blood seemed to freeze.

"You mentioned Ravensbrück in your talk," he was saying. "I was a guard there. . . . But since that time," he went on, "I have become a Christian. I know that God has forgiven me for the cruel things I did there, but I would like to hear it from your lips as well. Fraulein"—again the hand came out—"will you forgive me?"

There he stood, waiting for her response, while Corrie wrestled inwardly with "the most difficult thing I had ever had to do." She knew she must forgive him. But how? Only when she remembered that forgiveness is an act of the will, and not an emotion, did she attempt it. She prayed silently, "Jesus, help me! I can lift my hand. I can do that much. You supply the feeling." Corrie extended her hand, and I can't help but think that she was reaching for Jesus at the same time.

And as I did, an incredible thing took place. The current started in my shoulder, raced down my arm, sprang into our joined hands. And then this healing warmth seemed to flood my whole being, bringing tears to my eyes.

"I forgive you, brother!" I cried. "With all my heart."

For a long moment we grasped each other's hands, the former guard and the former prisoner. I had never known God's love so intensely as I did then. But even so, I realized it was not my love. I had tried, and did not have the power. It was the power of the Holy Spirit.[3]

In that moment, Corrie had seized God, and His healing, His power and His love, all at once. "And I pray that you, being rooted and established in love, may have power, together with all the Lord's holy people, to grasp how wide and long and high and deep is the love of Christ, and to know this love that surpasses knowledge—that you may be filled to the measure of all the fullness of God" (Ephesians 3:17–19).

Carolyn Weber sums it up so well: "*Carpe Deum* grasps at God. It seeks righteousness. It touches the robe. It holds onto the Lord and refuses to let go."[4]

SEIZE GOD'S STRENGTH

The other day, in one of my children's textbooks, I saw a painting depicting Moses holding up his arms during a battle, assisted by Aaron and Hur. Many artists have illustrated this moment from Exodus 17, but this painting, by John Everett Millais, is my favorite. You can see the exhaustion etching Moses's face, and it's evident in his posture as he sits on the rock. Verses 11–13 tell us that when Moses held his hands up, Joshua and his soldiers were winning the battle, but when Moses's strength flagged and his arms lowered, the Amalekites prevailed. With the help of Aaron and Hur, however, Moses kept his arms above his head, and Joshua and the Israelites won. God was their strength.

God has an endless supply of strength, and He loves to share it with His people. Isaiah 40:29 says, "He gives strength to the weary and increases the power of the weak." Psalm 29:11 is one of my favorite verses: "The LORD gives strength to his people; the LORD blesses his people with peace." In Ephesians 3:16, Paul writes, "I pray that out of his glorious riches he may strengthen you with power through his Spirit in your inner being."

When I don't want to seize the day, I can seize God's strength instead. My friend Susie Finkbeiner, a fellow novelist, says, "To me, *carpe Deum* means dropping the pretense that I can do anything on my own." (As the youngest of four siblings, she says she often falls into an "I can do it myself" mentality.) "I strive and struggle and dig myself into holes trying to succeed and accomplish and excel without any help," she told me. "That doesn't work so well."

But Susie says she can open her arms wide, "allowing God to fill in those cracks and gaps. While I can't possibly wrap my arms all the way around God—He's too vast, too great—I can seize Him within my being as He overflows in this cracked vessel of mine. I guess, really, that *carpe Deum* means allowing God to fully seize me in His merciful embrace."

The image of God cradling us in a fatherly embrace is shown in Scriptures like Psalm 91:4: "He will cover you with his feathers, and under his wings you will find refuge; his faithfulness will be your shield and rampart." What a comfort to know we can run to Him, leaning on His strength instead of our own. So many times, when all we want is to hide from our burdens, we find ourselves remarkably imbued with His strength instead.

In research for my Civil War novels and my nonfiction book *Stories of Faith and Courage from the Home Front*, I found numerous stories that proved this to be true. One of the most moving was that of a child who displayed supernatural strength when it was required of her.

Sadie Bushman was nine years old when the battle of Gettysburg broke out in a field between her home and her grandparents' house. She was running from one to the other when

> there came a screech and a shell brushed my skirt as it went by. I staggered from the concussion of it and almost fell, when I was grasped by the arm and a man said pleasantly, "That was a close call."
>
> "Come with me and hurry," he added in a tone so commanding that I meekly followed. [That man was Dr. Benjamin F. Lyford, a surgeon in the Union army.] He led me to . . . an army corps hospital and then he put me to work. Wounded and dying men were then being carried to the place by the score. . . .
>
> As I reached the hospital tent a man with a leg shattered almost to a pulp was carried in. "Give him a drink of water while I cut off his leg" was the command I got. How I accomplished it I do not know but I stood there and assisted the surgeon all through the operation. I was in that field hospital all during the three days of the battle, climbing over heaps of bodies six and eight deep and always with the doctor helping him in his work. Then my father found me and took me home.[5]

Sadie volunteered at a field hospital every day after that for five months. In the excerpt above, she admits she doesn't

know how she accomplished the work in that grisly environ-
ment. I can think of no other explanation but that God gave
that child a lion's share of strength when she needed it. He
can do the same for you and me.

SEIZE GOD'S LOVING GUIDANCE

The Gospels are full of Jesus's loving guidance. To His disciples,
He said, "Come, follow me" (Matthew 4:19). In Matthew 14,
He instructed His disciples to feed the five thousand, and then
after their work was done, put them on a boat for a peaceful
respite while He stayed behind and dismissed the crowd. He
even told Peter to walk on the water to meet Him (v. 29). To
the woman caught in the act of adultery, He said, "Neither do I
condemn you. . . . Go now and leave your life of sin" (John 8:11).

Each command from Jesus was for people's good, and
for God's glory. But nothing He asked was easy, in human
terms. For the disciples to leave behind everything they
knew—their families, their livelihoods, their homes—was no
small thing. Feeding the multitudes and walking on water?
Nothing short of miraculous. Even the adulterous woman
who was forgiven of her sins may have found it challenging
to forsake her sinful lifestyle.

And yet, who can deny the love Christ had for each of
them—and has for each of us? We may not understand where
He is leading us, or why. But we can always trust that He will
provide along the way, even when we're worn out and weary
from trying to go it alone. Let me share an illustration that
carries great weight personally.

I was working on Capitol Hill during the terrorist
attacks of September 11, 2001. Because I spent that day so

close to Washington's ground zero (ashes from the Pentagon floated in the air outside my house for three days), I pay special attention to other 9-11 stories. This letter from a New York City resident still brings me to tears:

> To the Police Officer who helped me on September 11th,
>
> You literally picked me up off the sidewalk that day. I was on the east side of City Hall Park and after the second WTC collapse I was running from the wall of dust and flying debris when I fell. I was terrified—people were running over me and past me. You lifted me off the ground and said "run with me." After a few blocks when I said I didn't think I could run anymore, you said run just a little further and then if you can't run I'll carry you. You got me to a safe place and went back to help others. I didn't get your badge number or your name but I will *never* forget you. I pray that you are safe. You and your brother and sister officers are one of the great things about this city.
>
> With love and gratitude,
> Ann (the lady in the gray dress and yellow sweater)[6]

This police officer's actions and words demonstrate God's attitude toward us: when we stumble in our own lives, our heavenly Father is unwilling to let us stay down. He picks us up and guides us to safety. When we cry out to Him that we just can't go on, He gently urges us to go further—and if we don't have the strength to carry on, He himself will carry us through.

Four times in his New Testament letters, the apostle Paul uses a "running the race" metaphor. And the writer of Hebrews puts the focus on endurance, indicating more of a marathon than a sprint: "Let us run with perseverance the race marked out for us, fixing our eyes on Jesus, the pioneer and perfecter of faith. For the joy set before him he endured the cross, scorning its shame, and sat down at the right hand of the throne of God. Consider him who endured such opposition from sinners, so that you will not grow weary and lose heart" (12:1–3).

When we're running our race—the one already decided upon and marked out for us by God himself—we must fix our eyes on Jesus. Not on the obstacles in our path, but on the One who can carry us through.

Carpe Deum. Seize God. Hold fast to Him and don't let go.

Seizing God in Moments Big and Small

For Catherine Fitzgerald, seizing God is a way of life that began when she was a child.

Her mother, as the family's primary breadwinner, left on Monday and returned on Friday of almost every week Catherine can remember. Her father, who stayed home, "did what he could in the midst of debilitating bipolar depression," she says. "Having a father who wasn't always there emotionally left a daddy hunger within me that led me to search for my Creator. I vividly remember of my first attempts at 'seizing God,' alone in my room where I spent much of my time, talking and conversing with this Being that I could not see, but knew to be true."

When adolescence hit, temptations and insecurities collided with family issues, sending Catherine into a tailspin. "After crashing and burning in ways I had vowed I never would, I found myself again reaching and grasping for a steady, immovable place and home—so I imperfectly seized God yet again."

Adulthood brought marriage and children—and the military. "Marrying a US Marine pilot sent me into a new town, away from everyone and everything I knew," she says. "The one expectation I had for marriage, to actually be with my husband, came crashing down. God began to reveal how I had turned so many things into idols to worship: my husband, my comfort, my plans. He slowly began to unclench my fingers from those things and my choice became clear. The only way I was going to make it through this life was by seizing God."

Catherine seized God in both small and big moments. "I seized Him when I was alone for the first time in a new place on my birthday while my husband was away for work," she says. "I seized Him when I had no friends or support system, hours away from home, after the birth of my first child. I seized Him after two miscarriages with a deployment on its heels. I seized Him as I waited and waited to get pregnant again. I seized Him when my husband was halfway across the globe, watching our son being born via Skype. I seized Him on those long and hard nights with a four-year-old and a newborn and a husband on an entirely different continent. I seized Him when my parents' tumultuous marriage finally reached its breaking point and they divorced."

Now, as the mother of three with a husband still in a military career, Catherine finds herself seizing God every day. "The fatigue of motherhood batters my soul. The fight for joy in the middle of diaper changes and sibling squabbles is a fight like none I've ever been in before. I'm seizing Him when I hold back from lashing out at a tired child, whose exhaustion manifests itself in a disobedient spirit and a spicy attitude. It's in the moment where through disheveled hair, wearing a shirt covered in snot and grubby fingerprints, I smile at my husband and offer him a warm hello after a hard day at work. It's in the moment where I put down my phone when everything inside of me screams to escape from the mundane and monotonous reality of life and instead be present in the moment with a little girl who found the most amazing lizard. Seizing God now comes in a much different form, and in some ways, a much richer one. But like most of us who have spent a lifetime trying to seize Him, you start to realize that in all those moments, big and small, it was less about you seizing Him and so much more about Him seizing you."

Your Turn

1. How can you invite God's presence into your day?
2. Does your self-talk match God's truth? If not, what verses can you claim to correct your thought patterns?
3. How can you seize God's strength today?
4. Do you have a harder time grasping God during large crises or daily trials? Why do you suppose that is?
5. As you're running your race, what would it look like for you to keep your eyes on Jesus?

Truths to Trust

Seizing God is more important than seizing the day. God is present in the small moments as well as in the big.

PART TWO

Pillars to Lean On

CHAPTER 6

Consistent Connections

"I am the vine; you are the branches. If you remain in me and I in you, you will bear much fruit; apart from me you can do nothing."

JOHN 15:5

Lord . . . Enable me to live so as to deserve a friend, and if I never have one on earth, be Thou my friend, for in having Thee I shall have all that is dear and valuable in friendship.

SUSANNA WESLEY
The Prayers of Susanna Wesley

If you watched the news as Hurricane Katrina ravaged the Gulf Coast in 2005, you likely recall the disturbing images of people stranded on their rooftops. Everything they had was underwater.

When I interviewed Lt. Iain McConnell, one of the Coast Guard helicopter pilots involved in emergency rescues, for a magazine article, I was shocked to hear him say this:

> On our first three missions, we saved the lives of eighty-nine people, three dogs, and a cat. On the fourth mission, to our great frustration, we saved no one—but not for lack of trying. The dozens we attempted to rescue refused pickup!
>
> Some people told us to simply bring them food and water. "You are trying to live in unhealthy conditions and the water will stay high for a long time," we warned them. Still, they refused. I felt frustrated and angry, since we had used up precious time and fuel, and put ourselves at risk during each rescue attempt. I felt like they were ungrateful. But, in truth, they did not know how desperate their situation was.[1]

A lifeline was dropped down to them, and they refused to take it.

As much as I shake my head at this, I recognize that I make the same mistake—every time I stubbornly try to live without connecting to the living lifelines within my reach.

REMAIN IN THE VINE

These days, Jesus doesn't show up in bodily form, holding out His hand to us. But His invitation is just as real, just as constant, and far more life-giving than any other.

Take a few minutes now to read John 15:1–17. In verse 5, Jesus says, "I am the vine; you are the branches. If you remain in me and I in you, you will bear much fruit; apart from me you can do nothing."

Humbling, isn't it? Without the Lord, we can stay busy, but we're spinning our wheels, not gaining any traction in the purposeful life He has for us. "I've been stretched to my max, physically and emotionally," my friend Krista told me, "But there is a difference between just being tired and that drained feeling that comes often times when you're not really plugged in with God and you're running on your own strength, like a hamster in a cage."

Let's take a look at just some of what God offers us when we abide in Him:

- love, joy, peace, patience, kindness, goodness, faithfulness, gentleness, self-control (Galatians 5:22–23)
- everything we need for a godly life (2 Peter 1:3)
- wisdom (James 1:5)
- strength (Psalm 29:11)
- living hope (1 Peter 1:3)
- grace (2 Corinthians 12:9)

Now think about your day. What difference would it make if you could have just a couple things from the list above? And yet, all of this *and more* is ours for the asking. It's overwhelming to me what we can have, if we do as Jesus says in John 15:9: "Now remain in my love."

What does it take to remain connected with God? Attending church services and gathering with other believers is vital. But in between those times, we can still nurture our personal relationship with God. As we discussed in Chapter 4, reading the Bible on your own and praying are great ways to know God better, and more easily discern His voice.

"I have to have that quiet time with God in the mornings," my friend Annabel told me. "But when I'm over-stressed, even my quiet time can stress me out—because I'm talking to God about all my stressors and it makes me feel even more stressed. That's a warning sign I'm doing something wrong. Praying should be casting my anxieties on Him, not just talking about them and then walking away with them still squarely on my shoulders. So I've had to be more cognizant of that—am I just thinking about my stress or am I actually praying?"

Throughout her day, Annabel now refers to note cards with specific Bible verses on them, "putting God's words in my mind, instead of having my quiet time be focused on my worries. I have to replace my worries with Scripture."

If you're in a season where sitting down to read for a dedicated period of time is unrealistic, get creative:

- Listen to the Bible while driving or cooking or folding laundry. Try a Bible reading/listening plan through YouVersion.com.
- Sign up for a daily email that sends Scripture to your in-box.

- Write Scripture verses on notecards or Post-its and put them up where you'll see them often.
- Choose a verse or passage to dwell on for the week. Keep a copy on your nightstand so you can read it before you get out of bed in the morning and before you turn out the light at night.
- If you have children in a church program like Awana, learn their assigned verses right along with them.

Praying, too, is an integral part of staying connected to the Vine. I love that Psalm 62:8 says, "pour out your hearts to him." That calls for much more than just mealtime blessings and bedtime prayers—it's a call for honest, open conversation anytime. We can pray on our knees, with our hands folded and heads bowed, or we can pray while driving, walking, or washing dishes. We can pray alone or corporately. When we're grateful or when we're spitting mad. The point is to simply keep talking to God.

Susanna Wesley, who mothered and educated ten children including John and Charles, the founders of Methodism, had a very distinctive prayer habit. In the midst of her crowded house, she would sometimes sit down and pull her apron over her head—the signal to everyone else to be quiet—so she could pray in peace.[2] I chuckle at this technique, but it worked!

If you don't have a dedicated time or space for prayer, and you aren't the hide-under-your-apron type, you can be creative with this, too. When my kids were younger and I felt like I was losing my self-control, I put yours truly into time-out so I could be alone to pray and recover my composure. (Is this any better than the apron?)

My friend Susie Finkbeiner likes "to pick a different color every once in a while, letting that color trigger in me praise as I go throughout my day. I believe in one-word prayers. While I might not be on my physical knees, I am doing my best to offer my heart to my almighty Father. I desire His will, His aid, His delight." Offering praise throughout her busy day, she told me, lends a perspective that helps ground her.

Our friend Amelia Rhodes decided to organize her friends' prayer requests by topic, and pray through them alphabetically. For example, A is for Adoption, B is for Bullying, and C is for Cancer. Focusing her thoughts by the letter allows Amelia to pray deeply for all those in her community facing similar issues. (Her method has since grown into a book, *Pray A to Z: A Practical Guide to Pray for Your Community*, which I recommend.)

As we lean into our purpose, we can say no to many things. Connecting to God, however, is not one of them. May we never be so busy serving Him that we don't take time to enjoy His presence. No matter what else is on your agenda, remain in God's love.

CONNECT TO COMMUNITY

It was a crisp September day in Vienna, Austria. Sunlight dazzled the mosaic tiles of the St. Stephen's cathedral roof, and its spire pointed to a brilliant blue sky. In the bustling square below, tourists in running shoes paused to watch street performers while locals sipped espressos at outdoor cafés. The scene was a page out of Fodor's travel guide.

And for me, it was just as two-dimensional. I was simply a spectator, unable to read, understand, or speak German.

Craving conversation, a human connection, I was left instead with a deafening silence.

Seeking post-college adventure, I had gone to Vienna to live with a family and teach their children English for the school year. I knew it would be hard, but in my pride of self-sufficiency, I wanted to prove just how independent I was. The language barrier, though, was too great, and my inability to connect with people banished me to isolation and then depression. Humans are wired for community—yes, even introverts like myself. And without it, I completely short-circuited. I returned home to the US before the snow fell, but it was months before I recovered my spirit.

Though Simon and Garfunkel's 1960s lyric "I am a rock, I am an island" is a classic, it was English poet John Donne who got it right more than three hundred years earlier when he wrote, "No man is an island, entire of itself; every man is a piece of the continent, a part of the main."

We *need* each other. We were designed for relationship not just with God but with our fellow men and women. "If one part suffers, every part suffers with it; if one part is honored, every part rejoices with it. Now you are the body of Christ, and each one of you is a part of it (1 Corinthians 12:26–27). To the Galatians, Paul wrote, "Carry each other's burdens, and in this way you will fulfill the law of Christ" (6:2). Right after Jesus told His disciples to remain in His love, He added, "Love each other" (John 15:12, 17).

None of this is possible in isolation. Whether we are single or married, introverted or extroverted, we all need consistent connection with people outside our own households, in ways that fit our current season of life. Even Susanna

Wesley asked God for a friend (see her quote at the beginning of this chapter).

When I'm stressed, I tend to keep my head down with laser focus, thinking the only thing that will help me feel better is to get my work done. But while a lack of progress never feels good, completely giving up relationships only leads to loneliness and isolation. I have been there before, and I don't want to go back to that place.

During a two-year period, Sarah Sundin navigated tighter-than-usual deadlines and some unexpected family events, including her daughter's wedding. "I stripped my schedule to the bone—no coffee with girlfriends, no book club, no leisurely shopping trips," she told me. "Other than work and family events, the only remaining activities were church and our small group Bible study. Even my women's Bible study, which I love, fell to the wayside most weeks. This worked, but it was a horrible way to live. I was stressed, and all my friends knew it. As a result, I made sure my new contract had more time between books. Life happens, and I need to make room for it."

When I was single and living in northern Virginia, I was very intentional about building community with friends outside of work and church. Now my life is radically different, but my need for connection remains. (A husband does not replace the companionship of girlfriends!) The key is figuring out what and how often is realistic. Sometimes the connection is making freezer meals with another mom instead of by myself. Other times it's a virtual coffee date via Skype with a long-distance kindred spirit, or dinner out with a friend while the kids stay home with their dads. Some seasons, one of my social highlights is getting my hair cut and talking to my stylist!

When it comes to friendships, what used to fit your schedule may not anymore. But are there opportunities you haven't considered? My friend Amber says, "I try to get a pedicure every two months. Last month, I was sitting in the salon with my feet in the soak tub and thought, *Maybe I should try to get a friend to come with me next time so I can connect with someone in addition to feeling better about my feet and my massaged legs.* So I'm going to try to do that more. I don't normally get to plan very far in advance, but I think I could try—and I think it might be a very worthwhile change."

My friend Mindelynn and I lived in the same wing of our college residence hall, but our friendship really bloomed years later, when we both worked in Washington, DC. I nicknamed her "The Great Connector" for the way she enthusiastically and consistently gathered people together socially. As I write this, she's a political consultant in Boston who still knows how to stay connected. She goes out for dinner and Red Sox games with friends, and vacations with them the week after elections. She uses FaceTime with her seven-year-old niece to discuss the American Girl books they're both reading for the first time. But when she's in the thick of an election cycle, on call twenty-four hours a day, every day of the week, her time isn't really her own.

"I'm deliberate about telling my friends to reach out to me during an election cycle, and I tell them what works," she told me. Mindelynn's friends know she won't be available to get together or talk much on the phone, but she does appreciate them checking in through email. "We don't like to tell people what we need, we like to provide. But during political campaigns, I can't provide the support. I need it."

Before Mindelynn shared this with me, it had never occurred to me to be intentional to that degree. Sure, I've notified friends and family of my crunch times, but it was more like, "You won't be seeing me or hearing from me for a while!" What if I went beyond that? What if we all did? During times when it's really easy to get wrapped up in our own work, at the very least we can still send the message that we need our friends—and would love to connect with them in some way, however briefly.

Most of the women I know would love more time for their friends than they can realistically fit in. If that's true for you, too, give yourself a break. Try something simple to connect:

- Instead of scrolling through social media sites, send an email to a friend and ask how you can pray for her.
- Invite a friend to join you in an activity that is already on your calendar—a pedicure, a freezer meal marathon, wrapping Christmas presents, or anything in between.
- Invite a friend to meet you either before or after an event you're both planning to attend, such as church service or a child's recital, so you can have a little one-on-one time.
- Send a new favorite recipe to a friend and ask for one of hers in exchange.
- Ask for help when you need it. You'd be surprised at the lengths your friends will go if they know that you need help. They probably miss you, too.

If I had known German while I lived in Vienna, I probably would have been much less of an "island." I'll never know for sure. But one thing I do know is this: I need people in my life. We all do.

SPEAK MY LANGUAGE

When I got home from Austria, I thought community would come automatically, because I speak the language. But since then I've learned, especially in my marriage, that it takes more than a mastery of English to communicate love. And the lessons I've learned apply to all relationships, not just those of a romantic sort.

Several years into my marriage, I was invited to co-author a military edition of *The 5 Love Languages* with Dr. Gary Chapman. I jumped at the chance, even though I hadn't yet read his original book cover to cover. When I did, in preparation for the military version, so many lightbulbs went off in my head it felt like a fireworks show. The book changed my life, and the way I relate to all my family members, overnight.

The premise of *The 5 Love Languages* is this:

1. The things that make you feel loved may not also help your spouse feel loved.
2. You can learn to love your spouse the way he or she can receive it.

So many women I've talked to have confessed they feel like they are shortchanging their husbands, and they want to fix that, but they don't know how—or feel they have the time. Here's the great news: once you learn how your spouse (or significant other, or family member) receives love, you can stop striving to show love in *all* ways because you'll be able to discern the *best* way. There is freedom here!

I highly recommend Dr. Chapman's book in its entirety, but I can't resist including a snapshot of it for you here. The five primary ways that people give and receive love, according to Dr. Chapman, are:

1. Words of affirmation
2. Quality time
3. Receiving gifts
4. Acts of service
5. Physical touch

From this list of love languages, one or two will usually communicate love to a particular person more than the other methods will. In a marriage relationship, it's rare that both spouses will speak exactly the same love language. And we tend to speak in the language that we like best, which is why it's so easy for disconnect to take place.

For example, my primary love language is quality time. I feel loved when I spend dedicated time with my husband. Rob's love language is acts of service. Now that we're aware of how we each feel loved the best, we work at speaking those languages. He spends time with me in the evenings, and I pack his lunch in the morning before work—not because I like it, but because he tells me that he feels loved when I do.

Knowing that my love language is quality time also helps explain why I can start to feel dejected when I'm on a deadline or when he's in grad school . . . or when both occur at the same time, like it is right now. We've learned that for our marriage to be healthy, the ideal circumstance is spending time together. But that isn't always realistic right now.

With time at a premium, we have to rely on other love languages. My secondary love language is words of affirmation. So when Rob tells me I'm doing a good job with the kids, or that he's proud of how hard I'm working to create something meaningful, or even that he *wishes* we could get away for a weekend together, I feel very loved.

Think about what it is that makes you feel loved. Is it encouraging words? Is it when you receive a gift? Is it through touch, or when someone does something kind or helpful for you in a very practical way? Now think through these same questions for your spouse or loved one. (If you need more clarity, take a free online quiz to find your love language at www.5lovelanguages.com/profile/.)

Here's where the freedom of this concept comes into play for your life. If your spouse's love language is quality time, let the housework go so you can spend time with him. If it's words of affirmation, speak genuine words of encouragement to him in person, or in an email or card. If it's acts of service, you might ask him which acts of service are most meaningful to him so you can focus your energies. While Rob loves his packed lunch, he seriously does not care how often I vacuum. And he would not feel loved at all if I decided to "serve" by rearranging the tools on his workbench. You get the idea—knowing how to express love effectively means we won't waste efforts that would be lost in translation.

Kathryn is another military wife I've kept up with over the years. She has two children with special needs, and was gracious enough to share her journey with me as I cowrote *Refresh: Spiritual Nourishment for Children with Special Needs*. With all the demands on her time, she still makes marriage a priority. She told me, "I don't let excuses prevent me from putting my spouse first. We make sure we have respite care and sitters we know and trust so we can go out and take a break one or two times a month. Without that, I think our marriage would have failed a long time ago. We both need that time. We also go to marriage counseling once a month. It helps so much because we can talk things through with our counselor and it helps us communicate so much better at home. What we've learned from counseling has changed and grown our marriage 100 percent."

Consistent connection with your loved ones will look different depending on several factors. The key is determining what works for your family in your current season and then making that a priority.

ON EMOTIONAL LEFTOVERS

Rob has low standards—for cooking, that is. As a bachelor, he often ate whatever he could prepare using a Mr. Coffee: ramen noodles, macaroni and cheese, and his all-time favorite, Stove Top Stuffing, just to name a few of his specialties. His favorite food? "Leftovers."

Since we've been married, I'm proud to say he's never eaten out of a coffee pot again. But, much to my relief, he is still an enthusiastic supporter of leftovers.

Unfortunately, the leftovers I serve Rob don't just come in the form of microwaved meatloaf or reheated rigatoni. More often than I care to admit, I give him my *emotional* leftovers, too. By the time he is done working for the day, I give him what's left of me—and after home-schooling two kids, maintaining the house, and trying to meet writing deadlines in between, that isn't as much as I'd like it to be.

Of course, one of the great things about being married is that you don't have to put on a happy face and turn on your charm every time you're around your spouse. We all have bad days (even just quiet days), and that's okay. When the emotional barrel is truly empty, love each other anyway. Remember, it's a choice, a commitment—not a feeling.

As women who lean, who work hard pouring ourselves into our purposes, it's easy to expend most or all of our energy during the day, leaving little for our spouses at the end. So what can we do about that?

Try these suggestions to keep emotional leftovers off the menu:

1. If something newsworthy or exciting happens during the day, think twice about telling the story several times to your friends or coworkers before you see your spouse again. With each re-telling, you may lose a degree of enthusiasm—and you want to give more than an abbreviated, watered-down account to your spouse.

2. Look for one thing every day that can make your spouse laugh, and share it in the evening.

3. If you have any control over your schedule, try not to do the most stressful tasks at the end of the day, right before you see your spouse again. That stress will easily spill over into your time together.

4. When you are truly spent at the end of the day, tell your spouse. Then describe what you need. For example, "Work was really stressful today, and I just need twenty minutes to myself to decompress. Then we can talk." Or, as I often say to Rob, "I used up all my words on the kids today, so I'm sorry I don't feel like saying much right now. But I would love to just listen to you share about your day."

5. If making dinner on a given day would really put you over the edge, pull out a frozen pizza or get carry-out instead. Some days it is worth the money to preserve your sanity so you can be emotionally present with your spouse.

6. Be careful about using Facebook or Twitter to instantly poll friends about a decision you need to make. Instead, take a moment to ask yourself if this is something to talk about with your spouse.

7. Surprise your spouse every once in a while with a favorite meal or an impromptu date night.

8. Recognize when your spouse needs a night for himself. Virtually always, if you give your spouse the freedom to do whatever he wants one night (whether that's watch a movie with friends, read a book in a coffee shop, or simply

go to bed early), he will be able to replenish the emotional reserves tank and want to spend time with you again soon.

9. Ask how you can pray for one another.

10. If you are perpetually serving emotional leftovers, be courageous enough, for the health of your marriage, to ask yourself if a lifestyle change is in order. Take a hard look at the stress factors and decide which ones you can decrease or eliminate.

We all have days that completely drain us, so it's inevitable that we will serve our spouses emotional leftovers from time to time. But with a little intentionality, an effort to save some energy for the most important ones in our lives, we can keep our marriages fresh.

As I finish this chapter, another hurricane is making headlines—this time, Hurricane Matthew. More emergency rescues are taking place. Disasters have a way of making us—most of us, anyway—reach for the lifelines that promise a connection to safety. May you and I both remember to stay connected to God, our communities, and our families, not just in times of crisis or when we think we have time to spare, but throughout every season. "My command is this: Love each other as I have loved you" (John 15:12).

Reaching Out to the Heart of God

Step inside Rebekah Benimoff's house, and you'll find Scripture posted on notecards in every room. "They're even in my car as visual reminders to invite God into my every day experience," she says. "To seek Him out, to seize Him, in the chaos *and* the calm; in the mundane, and the stressful, as well."

It's a battle strategy against an enemy who all too often throws flaming arrows of fear and anxiety at her areas of vulnerability. One of those arrows is the fear that a family member will die. "Having a son with a life-altering and sometimes life-threatening disease requires much fighting against the enemy's lies," she told me. "The enemy loves to use half-truths. The line he feeds us is so close to truth that it is believable. For example, it's true that my son could die from diabetes complications, if left untreated. But it's also true that with proper medical care, complications can be resolved. In every diabetic emergency, my peace of mind depends upon which truth I cling to—the enemy's version of it, or the truth of God that connects me to my Source and sets me free."

One day, the pump tubing to her son's body "kinked," blocking the insulin he needed. Without it, he began to experience extreme symptoms of diabetic ketoacidosis, prompting a trip to the emergency room so IV fluids could clear his body of dangerous ketones.

"I confess that I often experience high levels of anxiety during these emergencies," says Rebekah. "Sometimes I am literally fighting off panic as I drive my son to the ER . . . and once the rush to the hospital is over and he is admitted, medical personnel are streaming in and out of his room, I often find that my mind is still whirling, my heart is still racing. In those moments of waiting and hours of recovering, the battle to resist anxiety is on."

During these occasions, Rebekah usually handles the fear by requesting prayer on social media, and texting close friends and family members for support. "In these times, I often find myself looking for comfort in the reassurance of prayers going up on my son's behalf. Sometimes I am so busy seeking help from flesh and blood that I completely forget to reach out to the heart of God myself."

This last time, however, something was different. "For the past few weeks I've been studying the armor of God, and practicing being aware of the unseen battle— especially regarding my thought life. So, this time, I made a choice to seek connectivity to God and comfort from him—rather than relying on people. I still requested prayer on social media, because I believe that prayer is the most powerful tool we have—and when my son's well-being is at stake, I want all the prayer I can get."

"But this time," she continues, "instead of turning to the comment feed to soothe my racing mind, I opened my Bible app and sought truth. And I have to tell you that speaking Psalm 23 out loud over my son and myself was incredibly soothing. God's Word calmed me so much more than the many expressions of support from my friends and family. So, while I deeply appreciated the prayers and support going up on our behalf, this time, I chose not to lay my emotional stability upon them. Truth, as Paul tells us in Ephesians 6:14, when belted around our waists, stabilizes us. Truth holds *everything* together."

Your Turn

1. When you need help, who do you reach out for first?
2. What is one new way you can connect with God this week?
3. How can you reach out to a friend this week?
4. How do you think your closest loved one feels most loved? How can you express love in that way this week?
5. Of all the lifelines available to us—God, community, friends, family—which do you most often neglect to grab hold of? What would a realistic connection look like in that area?

Truths to Trust

Apart from God, we can do nothing.
We were built for community.

CHAPTER 7

Elastic Boundaries

*Like a city whose walls are broken through
is a person who lacks self-control.*

PROVERBS 25:28

*The most connected and compassionate people of those
I've interviewed set and respect boundaries.*

BRENÉ BROWN

*Daring Greatly: How the Courage to Be Vulnerable Transforms
the Way We Live, Love, Parent, and Lead*

For a while, everything was going well—at least from my perspective. I was leading a writers conference workshop on how to maximize writing time, and attendees were furiously scribbling notes, heads nodding. About halfway through, I used the phrase "be antisocial" to introduce my suggestion to curtail social media—in addition to phone calls, email, and visits—during time designated for writing. Not forever mind you, just during writing time.

That's when it all came to a screeching stop.

In the back of the room, a young woman stood up and cleared her throat. All heads turned as she addressed the group. "I just have to say something here," Lydia began. "Mrs. Green has written a lot of books, it's true. But *I* care about *people*." With a tear-choked voice, she went on to describe all the people that came to her for help and counsel, and how she never turned them away—because she cares.

As Lydia continued, it became clear that she was really saying that she cares and I don't. Caring people give themselves and their time freely, sacrificing their own work and goals, while only selfish people like me impose boundaries.

Whew. Try to segue out of that one.

Honestly, I feel for Lydia. Her heart is huge, and she wants to do the right thing for other people. She wants to serve. What's not to love about that? Yet, at the same time, there was a bitterness in her speech. The fact that she interrupted the workshop to defend her position tells me that, for better or worse, her open-door policy was a major deal in her life.

DEFINING OUR PROPERTY

Last month, the river that runs through our city's downtown reached record heights. In anticipation of imminent flooding, an emergency call for volunteers to sandbag was issued. Since the river is only seven blocks from our house, my kids and I walked down to the site while my husband coordinated volunteer efforts from his office. Others also streamed to the site, some on foot like us and some—college students from nearby universities—via school buses.

Once we were checked in, we got to work, filling, tying, and hauling sandbags to the top of the levee. Our wall of sandbags drew a bright orange line which said to the river, "You may come so far, but this side belongs to us." The boundary defined our communal property—our downtown Main Street—and protected it.

This is what boundaries do for us. They are the fences we build around what is precious to us. They protect what we have, so it's not washed away.

Boundaries are about far more than just "saying no." Boundaries define who we are and who we are not. They establish what is our responsibility and what is *not* our responsibility. They help us to be accountable for our own lives, and not anyone else's. In other words, we are responsible for our own words, actions, decisions, behavior. But we are not in charge of how others respond.

Boundaries are not meant to wall us off from the rest of our community. In John 17:11, Jesus prays for His disciples in this way: "Holy Father, protect them by the power of your name, the name you gave me, so that they may be one as we are one." If we are one as the Trinity is one, we experience unity while we are still allowed our separateness—just as God the Father, God the Son, and God the Holy Spirit, though one, are three distinct Persons.

Having clear boundaries does *not* mean we only look out for ourselves. Galatians 6:2 says, "Carry each other's burdens, and in this way you will fulfill the law of Christ." Dr. Henry Cloud and Dr. John Townsend explain what this verse means:

> Many times others have "burdens" that are too big to bear. They do not have enough strength, resources, or knowledge to carry the load, and they need help. Denying ourselves to do for others what they *cannot* do for themselves is showing the sacrificial love of Christ. This is what Christ did for us. He did what we could not do for ourselves; he saved us. This is being responsible "to."
>
> On the other hand, verse 5 says that "each one should carry his own load." Everyone has responsibilities that only he or she can carry. These things are our own particular "load" that we need to take daily responsibility for and work out. No one can do certain things *for* us. We have to take ownership of certain aspects of life that are our own "load." . . .
>
> Problems arise when people act as if their "boulders" are daily loads, and refuse help, or as if their "daily loads" are boulders they shouldn't have to carry. The results of these two instances are either perpetual pain or irresponsibility.[1]

By "problems," the authors refer to a host of symptoms. "Depression, anxiety disorders, eating disorders, addictions, impulsive disorders, guilt problems, shame issues, panic disorders, and marital and relational struggles, find their root in conflicts with boundaries."[2]

ARE BOUNDARIES BIBLICAL?

The concept of boundaries is not just a pop-culture self-help trend, but relies on wisdom that is solidly biblical. Consider the following passages.

- The parable of the ten bags of gold in Matthew 25:14–30 illustrates God-ordained responsibility for ownership and use of talents. We are accountable to God to use our resources effectively.
- "Each of you should give what you have decided in your heart to give, not reluctantly or under compulsion, for God loves a cheerful giver" (2 Corinthians 9:7). Though this verse refers to money, it also applies to our other resources of time and energy. According to the apostle Paul, *we* get to freely decide what we want to give. If we give out of guilt, we'll become resentful.
- "Like a city whose walls are broken through is a person who lacks self-control" (Proverbs 25:28). Self-control is a form of internal boundaries, which we'll talk about later. (Notice that nowhere in the Bible is a reference to "other-control." We are to take responsibility only for ourselves.)

An Opportunity Is Not Necessarily God's Open Door

I so appreciate this insight from my friend Kathy Collard Miller, author of Never Ever Be the Same. *Hear what she has to say about Jesus's example for us.*

As I visited with my friend who complained about everything going on in her life and all she felt compelled to do, I could sense she expected me to volunteer to help. My heart went out to her but I'd really been seeking God's will rather than responding to every need of others. It took every fiber of my trust in God to *not* offer to take some of the load from her—but in my heart, I knew God wasn't calling me to this particular need.

Although I still succumb at times to the pressure of others' needs, I've come a long way in learning to seek God first. A major help was seeing Jesus's response to needy people. Of course, He healed the needy people clamoring for His help, but I also remind myself of a curious passage of only two verses that we could easily overlook. It's Luke 5:15–16: "But the news about Him [Jesus] was spreading even farther, and great multitudes were gathering to hear Him and to be healed of their sicknesses. But He Himself would often slip away to the wilderness and pray."

If Jesus had wanted to set an example of selflessness by doing everything everyone wanted, He wouldn't have left that needy group behind. They wanted Him to stay with them and meet all their needs. Instead, He needed to spend time with the Father—and He did. I can just imagine their disgruntled comments as He walked away. "Oh, He says He's the Messiah, huh? Well, if He is, why isn't He healing me? Why isn't He showing His power to me? He must not be any kind of God at all." But Jesus was not swayed by their needs, opinions, or demands. He risked His reputation before others—and His heavenly Father's. Instead, Jesus never responded to human need; He responded to what He saw His Father doing and prompting Him to do. Although He obviously felt compassion for all people, He didn't respond automatically; He responded out of obedience to God.

That is why I remind myself, and sometimes others: An opportunity is not necessarily God's open door. Just because we hear of a need, though it may seem that we need to be selfless, it doesn't necessarily mean God wants us to respond. Just as Jesus listened intently to the voice of His Father and obeyed what His Father wanted Him to do, we must seek God's direction and only do what He wants us to do, regardless of what others think of us.

Yes, to do that, we face a great challenge when we try to hear and know what service God wants us to do. Our own mixed motives and wrong ideas can make it difficult to be sure. We must recognize our tendency to justify our selfishness, as well as our habits of feeling responsible for the choices and decisions of others. We are not at the mercy of everyone who desires our time, efforts, or money. Jesus wasn't because He trusted the Father's plan—even if it meant leaving needy people behind. We can have the same confidence, even when we are misunderstood. God may not use us but He promises He'll meet the real needs of every person calling upon Him (Philippians 4:19).

WE BUILD OUR OWN

One difference between our boundaries and the sandbag walls volunteers built to protect our town is this: we're the only ones who can build our own boundaries. No one else will do that for us.

We have to be the ones to govern our own lives, to take responsibility for how we use our resources. And then we must take that next critical step of communicating our choices to others. No one is going to read our minds and divine where our boundaries are (1 Corinthians 2:11). It's up to us to make them clear—whether we're protecting our time, our emotions, our energy, or our money. Listen in as five of my friends share how they've done this.

Charlotte: I have refused to spend a significant amount of time outside of work working. For the most part my evenings and weekends are spent with my family. However, this has resulted in my being "less productive" at work, because the expectation is that we are to do research and other academic activities outside our regular work schedule. As a result of not having enough research or publications, my job was changed and an area of my work that was very meaningful to me was given to someone else. I was told that when this other person was hired, she was going to be great because she "wasn't married and didn't have kids." That was a rough time for me, but I don't regret my decision to protect my time at home.

Cynthia: A mentor once told that "a no inside is a no outside." I've used this to coach myself many a time. I feel like I can ask people things because I trust they can say no to me, too.

Being differentiated from others and their expectations has been freeing for me. When I was doing my degree and teaching full time, a colleague wanted me to serve on her committee, which I declined, explaining why. She chided me, which didn't bother me. I thought, No way!

Grace: I find I must be strict about setting boundaries with people who want to "catch up" with me. They'll say, "Let's get together for an hour," but it always turns into more than that. I will (1) set an appointment with a scheduled start and finish time near the end of the afternoon so I have a large chunk of focused time during the day ("I'm available from 4–5 p.m. next Monday. Does that work for you?") or (2) set up a lunch date with them at a favorite restaurant if this person is more than a mere acquaintance.

Sharron: Right around the time I turned forty I began leading a large ministry and conducting training for leaders. A module I added was dedicated to teaching how and why to set boundaries, and offering some language to say no. I had learned to say, "I am honoring my time with my family, and I just can't take on another commitment." It's pretty tough for someone to argue with a commitment to honor family. Some will, but most won't. Some will say, "The work I am asking you to do is honoring to God." But it is not honoring God to neglect your family.

Janet: I live in a small community and many my age are retired. Because I work out of our home, most people don't understand that I'm actually "working"—so I'm often invited out to lunch or to play bunko in the middle of the day. I have to explain that those kinds of activities eat into my day—by the time I get ready, go there, and get back, I don't feel like working.

People do try to make me feel guilty or that I'm being snobbish, but I don't receive it or let it bother me. I'm as kind as I can be with my explanations. Since I love walking in the morning, I'll invite anyone who wants to spend time with me to come walk and talk with me—but few take me up on that offer.

"Every limit is a beginning as well as an ending," wrote Mary Ann Evans, better known by the pseudonym George Eliot, in the final chapter of her novel *Middlemarch.* How true this is of boundaries! When we define what we won't do, it allows us to do what God has purposed us to do at home and in work. A limit on one thing is the beginning of another.

OWNING OUR FEELINGS

Before we can communicate our limits to others, we must define and practice internal boundaries. The renewing of our minds (Romans 12:2) and the call for self-control (Proverbs 25:28) refer to our thoughts and attitudes, which will, in turn, spill over into our behavior.

Years ago, when my colicky newborn was crying and my toddler was throwing a temper tantrum, I frankly felt like joining in. I remember very clearly grabbing the edge of the changing table, closing my eyes and repeating, "Dear Lord, please help me to be more emotionally mature than my two-year-old right now." I'm sure it was quite a scene, since I had to say the prayer loudly enough to hear it over my wailing children! But it worked. I was reminded that my response is not dictated by those around me. I'm still in charge of myself.

Earlier in this chapter, I shared about Lydia, who stood up in my workshop and tearfully confessed she wasn't progressing toward her own goals because she "cares too much about people." Later that day, I sat down with her. As she stirred sugar into her tea, she told me that her writing was at the mercy of everyone else who asked for her time. This is what happens in a boundary-less life. Lydia was so afraid of hurting others that she always gave herself away. But at the same time, she blamed *them* for her not getting her work done. And she harbored resentment toward me for accomplishing my own goals.

Listen—people will make demands on your time. That is up to them. And it is up to you to answer. We can't blame anyone else for how *we* respond to them. Lydia's refrain was, "I can't work because all these people keep coming to me." But it would be more accurate for her to say, "I'm *not* working because *I keep saying yes* to all these people."

We're not powerless. Between a request and our response there is a space. In that space we have the freedom to choose how we respond, both in thought and deed. Always, our actions follow what's in our hearts (Luke 6:45). So let's examine our hearts.

HEART CONDITIONING

Have you ever noticed how often women apologize when they can't meet—or choose not to meet—an expectation? See if any of these examples sound familiar:

> "I'm sorry, but I can't go to that event."
> "I'm sorry it's taken me this long to return your phone call."
> "Sorry the house is a mess."
> "I'm sorry I'm crying."
> "I'm sorry—I don't like green peppers on my pizza."

I've said all of these things, among countless other unnecessary expressions of apology. We should say "I'm sorry" when we have hurt, slighted, or offended someone, right? And yet think about all the times we apologize for things that do not warrant it. I'm training myself not to start my sentences with "I'm sorry" unless I'm actually apologizing for doing something wrong.

Or we say, "I'm afraid"—as in, "I'm afraid that won't work out for me." Really? It might soften the sound of "can't" or "won't," but it also communicates fear. What are we afraid of? We're afraid of other people's reactions. Maybe they will be disappointed with us. Maybe our deepest fear is that they won't even like us anymore.

Recognizing your boundaries should release you from that fear, and from the false guilt that prompts you to apologize. You are responsible for making the right decision—you are not responsible for how anyone responds to your decision. That does not fall within your area of ownership. Other people's feelings are their own property, not yours. (Read those lines again if you need to. I hope you sense the freedom in this truth!)

I first became acquainted with Colleen Saffron when we were volunteer leaders together with the online ministry Christian Military Wives. She went to school for design and receives many requests for her skills—but not everyone is willing to pay for her services. "Boundaries are harder to maintain as people get offended when you don't want to give them a 'freebie,'" she told me, "but honestly, people who want my time, creativity, and effort for free are not valuing me or my abilities. I had to let go of feeling guilt for other people's lack of respect for others."

As the caregiver for her veteran husband, Colleen also wisely crafted a mission statement to help her sort through what is her responsibility and what isn't. "I had to," she said. "It's very easy to cross the line from caregiving to enabling.

With brain injuries it is very hard to know what the injury is and what a stubborn husband is. I had to learn to not be so emotionally attached to his problems. They are not caused by me and I cannot fix them. I can empathize without being too responsible for his feelings."

As a self-proclaimed people-pleaser, PeggySue Wells had a habit of spontaneously saying yes and volunteering for everything. That is, until the day she crawled into bed and pulled the covers over her head in despair because she had taken on more than was physically possible to accomplish. Her perspective on her own heart condition is insightful:

> I learned that as a people-pleaser I was the most self-centered of people. I did things to "please" others so others would give me the acceptance, approval, attention, and appreciation I craved. In other words, my actions were to manipulate others to give me what I wanted from them. Ouch! Then if someone did not respond with what I expected from them, I was offended. Expectations are offenses waiting to happen. None of it was honest, nor are people supposed to fill my needs or expectations.
>
> As I shifted into being personally responsible for my emotions, needs, and results, I had healthier relationships. When I learned how much God loves me and that His plans for me are awesome, I learned to listen to His voice and His guidance. Now I say I will pray about a request for twenty-four hours before giving an answer.

Following God's guidance in what I do and don't do is a place of rest, security, belonging, and freedom for me and those around me. When I play to an audience of *One*, I am authentic and secure. Then I love others through Him.

I find it so interesting that Brené Brown, in all her research on shame, vulnerability, and wholeheartedness, discovered that the most connected and compassionate people were those who set and respect boundaries. But it only makes sense. When you "give what you have decided in your heart to give, not reluctantly or under compulsion" (2 Corinthians 9:7), you're not giving out of guilt or fear. You're not giving from a false self as you strive to please people, but from a place of authenticity, after careful decision. You own your choice—it wasn't made for you.

BOUNDARIES THAT MOVE

Recently, with my input, my husband created a chart called Family StressCon, short for "stress condition." (What do you mean you can tell he's a former military officer who creates strategic planning graphics for fun?) The chart has five rows—one each for StressCon—Normal, Alpha, Bravo, Charlie, and Delta, the latter being the most stressed out we could ever be and remain alive. There are also columns describing each StressCon level, and what is appropriate for each in the discretionary categories of Hospitality, Dining, Household, and Entertainment.

StressCon Alpha, our default setting, indicates minor stress from work or grad school. Here's how its categories break down:

- **Hospitality:** Playdates and dinner guests encouraged.
- **Dining:** Home cooking four times a week or more. Baking encouraged.
- **Household:** Regular yardwork and gardening. Uniform: daily wear. Regular hygiene expected.
- **Entertainment:** Family movie nights and game nights encouraged, no multi-tasking. Netflix-watching allowed after kids go to bed. Special events and trips allowed.

As you move down the chart, through StressCon Bravo, Charlie, and Delta, the boundaries constrict tighter and tighter. During StressCon Charlie (a close-at-hand book deadline or grad school finals), we will only have relatives in the house, though meeting people for dinner outside our home is fine. I also only cook twice a week, including re-heating freezer meals. The uniform includes couch pants. (StressCon Delta is a place we hardly ever want to be. Think paper plates and plastic silverware. Also, hygiene is unlikely.) Rob and I also defer to the one who has more stress. So if I'm at Bravo and he's at Charlie, the entire family operates under StressCon Charlie. We're on the same page—that is, the same row of the chart.

As unusual as Rob and I may be, we've found this to be really helpful. It means we don't have to spend energy deliberating on some daily and weekly choices. (Should Jocelyn bake cookies today? Chart says buy them instead! Could Rob have someone from work over for dinner? Chart says eat out instead! Have a great time!) It helps us to clearly communicate expectations.

Not every family will enjoy this kind of thing as much as we do. But having some clear policies in place for the family saves energy that would otherwise be used in making the same types of decisions over and over. For example, before the crunch occurs, you can set a limit on the number of Christmas parties or events you want to attend every December, or make a policy on specified blocks of time for rest or family activities.

We still own our charted boundaries; they don't own us. Which means we move the boundaries to allow for situations we don't want to decline, even when time is at a premium. It's my niece's birthday? Forget the chart, let's party! A family member or friend is truly in need with a burden beyond their daily load? Forget the chart, how can I help?

Establishing boundaries is helpful and necessary, as long as we remember to keep them elastic, not rigid. We must pay careful attention to the Holy Spirit—God always trumps the chart. We have our guidelines in place, but we make exceptions, too. We obey the daily call to Christlike living as much as we invest in our big-picture purpose.

Boundaries can change with your season of life, even your day-to-day activities. Learning where and when to draw the line—and when to move it—is key.

Shannon Popkin admits this is an area in which she struggles. "I don't draw clear boundary lines, so my work bleeds into other areas of life," she told me. "I spend too much time trying to finish my projects, and I'm not as open as I should be to interruptions." Those interruptions, though, especially by her kids, can be valuable. "We have a couch in our office, and one of the kids will often wander in and sit down when I'm working at the computer. This is my cue that they have a question or they're working through something. These moments are a fleeting gift, and I want to be fully present as a parent; not distracted or thinking about the e-mail or blog comment that I'd like to get back to.

Some interruptions, even from our kids, can and should be deferred, especially when their idea of a "necessary" interruption is asking who I'd rather fight, a bear with shark arms or a shark with bear arms. (True story.) Yet some interruptions are invitations to stop what we're doing and pay attention to something even more important. It takes discernment to know the difference.

Productivity for its own sake is not our ultimate goal. Our aim is to know God and follow His leading. Some days—or for some of us, many days—He may lead you a fair distance away from your to-do list. But our families and our own health are among the things He's given us to steward well. Boundaries aren't all about saying no—they help us take ownership of that which is truly our responsibility, not just what we do, but who we are.

Who You Are Matters

For years, Tonya said yes. But most people didn't realize that though she was good at the things she poured herself into, more and more of her own spirit drained away each time.

"I feel especially obligated to say yes to family and church commitments," she admits. "That's my weakness, especially if the person asks me when we are face-to-face. Busy events with large crowds exhaust me to the point that I can get physically ill, but I'm good at coordinating and hosting such events. So I say yes, and then I regret it. And my husband asks why I ever agreed to do it."

Part of the trouble was that Tonya "fell into the trap of believing that doing 'good' things was what God rewarded, that self-sacrifice was what a Christian life was all about. It made me miserable—and often ill—but I did it."

Things came to a crisis point after her brother-in-law died and left behind a wife and children. "I broke," she says. "I poured myself out pleasing everyone else. They were all hurting so badly and I wanted to help. But I didn't take care of myself. What had been a lifelong philosophy of self-sacrifice escalated into a real problem. I started having terrible panic attacks."

Fortunately, she was already seeing a good counselor who was not affiliated with her church or family. "He asked me, 'Who is Tonya?' Tears still come to my eyes when I recall not being able to answer that question. He pressed the issue, saying, 'Not who your husband thinks you are, or your parents. Who you really are, on the inside.' I had never realized that it mattered who I was. I would sometimes feel frustrated when people wouldn't understand me and yet I was unconsciously feeding the problem."

Defining who she was—and who she wasn't—proved to be a life-changing process which led to her going to college and pursuing a teaching career in a private school. "God is using my failings and my mistakes to shape me and grow me," she says. "You see, by saying yes to the 'good' things, I was missing out on the 'great' things. I am terrified of both teaching and returning to college, yet if these are some of the 'great' things, how can I tell God no?"

Tonya's breakdown led to her breakthrough, which helped her see that her daughter, too, needed help. "She was trying to care for her cousins and her father and her grandparents at a great cost to herself," Tonya recalls. "Because I had been there myself, I recognized the signs when she walked out of ballet and said she couldn't go on any more. We pulled her out of ballet and cancelled school for a few weeks—I love homeschool for that. She literally laid on the couch for most of the time."

Gradually, Tonya's daughter recovered her spirit, and has thrived. "She has taught herself to make candy, to compose songs by ear on the piano, and to skateboard. She also found that she has a real talent and passion for graphic design—a career option she didn't even know existed before. God is using this hard time to grow her into a wonderful young woman."

These days, Tonya seeks God's guidance first when making decisions and strives to follow His example. "In the end, I have to depend on Him to make good come out of my mistakes," she says. "He has used my mistakes to teach me so much that I have to believe He will continue to do so."

Your Turn

1. What areas of life do you need to take better responsibility for? What kind of boundaries can you place around them? Are there any boundaries you need to communicate more clearly to others? How will you do this?
2. When was the last time you gave reluctantly or out of compulsion? What happened?
3. If you agonize over how others will respond to your choices, what can you tell yourself to boost your confidence?
4. Next time someone tries to make you feel guilty for something, how will you respond, either mentally or verbally?

Truths to Trust

We are responsible for our own choices.
We are not responsible for how others respond to our choices.

CHAPTER 8

Breathing Room

*"Come to me, all you who are weary and burdened,
and I will give you rest."*

MATTHEW 11:28

*Never is a woman so fulfilled as when she chooses to underwhelm
her schedule so she can let God overwhelm her soul.*

LYSA TERKEURST
The Best Yes: Making Wise Decisions in the Midst of Endless Demands

I could have melted into the pavement as the police officer turned a withering glare on me. Not that I didn't deserve it.

"You're not from around here," he stated. "What are you doing in these parts?"

Sheepishly, I told him, "I was speaking at the Friends of the Library appreciation tea." In a severely sleep-deprived state. Then I had gotten back into my minivan and started the long drive home from this small Iowa town. I suppose I should also tell you that I rear-ended the car in front of me near an intersection. (I tried leaving that part out, by the way, but the story doesn't make as much sense without it. Drat.)

It could have been worse. I was stopped in a line of cars behind a red light. When the light turned green, the car in front of me started moving, and I lifted my foot off the brake. But then I reached for the map on the passenger's seat, so I didn't see that the car in front of me had stopped again, waiting to turn left into a gas station. *Bam!* I rolled right into her.

Completely, undeniably my fault. I was shaken, not only by what I had done but by how much worse it could have been.

When I finally got home, Rob asked me, "Are you okay?"

"No," I sobbed into my hands. "I am not okay." I'd been running on fumes for weeks and couldn't see how I could stop running unless I crashed—metaphorically and literally.

That month was a perfect storm of commitments. I was still trying to finish my novel *Yankee in Atlanta* after getting a three-week deadline extension. The problem was that I'd also scheduled a number of speaking engagements after my original deadline, thinking I would have plenty of time. So now I was speaking when I needed to be writing. The release of *The 5 Love Languages Military Edition,* which I co-authored with Dr. Gary Chapman, was that same month, requiring several radio interviews. (Also, insert raising children here.) I was more than maxed out.

I was desperate. I felt like I could barely breathe.

BURNED OUT FOR JESUS?

I'm not proud of my cautionary tale, and yet God has used that miserable experience to teach me what I'd lost sight of: neglecting the needs of my body and spirit is never the right solution.

Neglecting the needs of *your* body and spirit is never the right solution.

As Tonya shared in her story at the end of Chapter 7, the idea of self-sacrifice is so ingrained in many of us that it's easy to take it beyond what Christ expects. Yes, we are to take up our cross and follow Him (Matthew 16:24), and He may ask us to work hard and sacrifice some comfort and convenience as we fulfill His purpose for us. But do we really believe that when we follow Jesus, He'll lead us through a meat grinder?

When I worked at a nonprofit in Washington, DC, some of my friends worked for their congressional representatives. The chiefs of staff worked these fresh college graduates as though they were disposable. After all, there was always a long line of applicants ready and eager to replace them, hungry for a Capitol Hill position to add to their resumés. Hill staff went through recent grads like Kleenex, using them up and tossing them out in no time.

God doesn't work that way. You are not disposable. You cannot be replaced by anyone else, and God does not treat you as though you should be. You're unique, and you are loved beyond comprehension. We get to serve God not because He needs us to—He created the universe quite well without us—but because He wants us to enjoy the privilege of being part of His work on earth. God is never so desperate for our human efforts that He drives us to the breaking point.

We do that on our own just fine, don't we?

No one intentionally drives her car until she runs out of gas on the highway and then says, "Look what a dedicated driver I am! I have absolutely nothing left to give. This is commitment, right here." No one routinely spends every dime she has between paychecks and then says, "I'm completely broke! Wiped out, again. Just goes to show how good I am at spending everything I have." No—the average, sane person leaves a reserve. But when it comes to our spirit and our energy? Not so much.

Do you ever get the feeling that pushing forward through times of stress is greatly admired in our culture, but that carving out time for yourself is seen as weakness? Me, too. And while there is a lot to be said for perseverance, a little more could be said for breathing room.

You already know I've struggled with this. So as you read this chapter, please understand I'm not on a pedestal, preaching with pointed finger. If you're in the trenches right now, picture me there with you—one arm around your shoulders, pointing to the light above us, whispering, "There is light, we don't have to stay here." If you are flat on your face on the floor, picture me right there with you, among the Cheerios and Goldfish crackers ground into the carpet, ignoring the smell of the overflowing Diaper Genie nearby. This chapter is me saying, "Come on, sister. We'll belly crawl out of here together. We don't have to stay here."

The Lord is our shepherd. He makes us lie down in green pastures, He leads us beside quiet waters, He refreshes our souls. When we're not too busy to let Him.

THE BUSY BUG

In the 1960s, futurists predicted that one of the biggest problems for future generations would be what to do with all our spare time, given our time-saving devices. In fact, in 1967, a testimony before a Senate subcommittee claimed that by 1985, people could be working just twenty-two hours a week, or twenty-seven weeks a year, or could retire at age thirty-eight.[1]

I'll give you a moment to laugh.

I wonder what those futurists would say about how we're living today. About half of Americans who work fifty or more hours per week don't take the vacation time they've earned.[2] Americans guzzle coffee and energy drinks to power through the day, then need sleeping pills to help shut them down for the night. Around the world, people are even walking faster than they used to.[3] There's just no way to calculate the family, church, and community activities filling our calendars. Progress, as it turned out, hasn't saved us time—instead, it gives us more and more of everything, at a pace we can barely keep up with.

Busyness has become a badge of importance and worthiness. A breakneck speed might be commended by the world. But the same person who seems like she's "on fire!" may be simultaneously burning out.

"Though it feels like we gain a little extra distance or traction in the moment when we pick up speed and keep our foot on the pedal for an extended period of time, in reality we lose ground when we live like this," writes Susie Larson. "When we try to run a marathon at sprint pace, we miss life, the life God intended for us, and we can't possibly savor the sacred sweet journey up mountains, through valleys, and by still waters."[4]

Not all busyness is a sign that our life is in need of an overhaul. Some people have greater capacity than others to be very productive without being overly stressed. Discerning the difference between un-appointed busyness and God-ordained fruitfulness, Larson says, is a matter of looking at the fruit.

> Has all of your output left you with an increased sense of expectancy and wonder?
>
> Have you seen God take your offering and multiply it in a way that is beyond you? Do you see your fruit bearing more fruit? . . . Stay the course. Trust His love. And do what He says. He'll guide your every step. . . .
>
> Though we may battle weariness on occasion, God's yes for us will not grind our gears, wear us out, or keep us running at a sprint as a way of life. Jesus doesn't want to burn us out; He wants us to finish strong.[5]

Even when God is blessing us with fruitfulness, however, we still need to take care of ourselves. No one else will do that for us.

OUR RESET BUTTON

For many of us, sleep is among the first things we cut out when we're crunched for time. Of course, we lose sleep for all kinds of reasons that aren't really within our control: a newborn baby needs to be fed, or a child gets the flu, or we have an early flight to catch, or (you fill in the blank). But, as a general rule, sleep is something we should consider non-negotiable.

God created us with a need to sleep. It's part of His perfect design for us. When He called man and woman "very good" at the point of Creation, that pronouncement included even our human limitations. The fact that God divided day from night leads me to believe that sleep was part of the human experience even before the Fall in Genesis 3. These are the parameters of life, not indications of weakness. Listen to this: "In vain you rise early and stay up late, toiling for food to eat—for he grants sleep to those he loves" (Psalm 127:2).

During sleep, our bodies repair and replenish in ways they can't when we're awake. Sleeping improves the immune system and contributes to restorative functions in muscle growth and tissue repair, the synthesis of proteins into our bodies, and hormone regularity. It's also believed that sleep is related to memory function as well, aiding in the consolidation and storage of new information and experiences so we can recall them at a later time. (That is enough for me to call sleep a productive task!)

People who regularly sleep less than six hours a night are more likely to:

- **Gain weight.** Sleep duration affects hormones regulating hunger and appetite. Plus, when we're tired, we're less likely to exercise. According to Mayo Clinic, women who slept less than six hours a night were more likely to gain weight compared to those who slept seven hours a night.[6]
- **Get sick and stay sick longer.** Sleep deprivation decreases the production of certain protective proteins that are produced during sleep. Infection-fighting antibodies are also reduced when we don't get enough sleep.[7]
- **Develop diabetes.** Insufficient sleep may lead to type 2 diabetes by influencing the way the body processes glucose. Adults who usually sleep less than five hours per night have a greatly increased risk of having or developing diabetes.
- **Develop coronary heart disease.** According to Harvard Medical School, sleeping less than six hours increased the risk of coronary heart disease in women.[8]
- **Forget things and be distracted.** Not sleeping enough decreases your ability to concentrate and learn new things. Both short-term and long-term memory suffer, and your exhausted brain has trouble making decisions and being creative.[9]
- **Be irritable.** We've all been there. Sleep deprivation makes it difficult to cope with even minor annoyances. Short tempers and mood swings are likely.
- **Get in a car accident.** (Ouch.) Drowsy driving is as dangerous as drunk driving.[10]

The list goes on, but I'll let you Google the rest if you need more reasons to take sleep seriously. Research abounds. Our bodies must have sleep to function the way God meant them to.

Sleep is also God's way of telling us every day that we need to stop. That the world will go on without us, that we're truly human and not divine beings. We have limits we must respect. Those limits force us to prioritize what we will do in this day, and what can wait for another. When we sleep, we can trust God to handle all that concerns us even without our "help."

Sleep is our reset button, and I'm so thankful for that. Then when we wake up? God's mercies, or compassions, have reset all over again for the coming day: "His compassions never fail. They are new every morning" (Lamentations 3:22–23).

Good Night, Sleep Tight!

Try these tips for a better night's rest.

1. Get on a sleep schedule. Going to bed and waking up at the same time every day reinforces a consistent sleep-wake cycle.
2. Limit your caffeine intake during the day. Cut yourself off as early as you need to in the afternoon so it doesn't interfere with your ability to wind down at night.
3. Make your bedroom a work-free zone. You want to send signals to your body that when you're in the bedroom, it's time to sleep.

4. Create a bedtime ritual to help train your body to wind down. Try a hot shower or bath, relaxing music, or reading a book with lights dimmed. Avoid screens during this time, as some research suggests electronic devices just before bed interfere with sleep.

5. Be comfortable. If you have a terrible mattress, invest in a new one that suits you. If noise or light is a problem, consider ear plugs, an eye mask, room-darkening blinds, a fan or white noise. Wear comfy pajamas!

6. Exercise during the day. Physical activity can improve sleep quality, as long as you don't do it just before bedtime.

7. Pray. Hand over all that worries to you to the One who never sleeps. "He who watches over you will not slumber" (Psalm 121:3).

If you struggle with poor quality sleep on a regular basis, see your doctor for other ideas.

THE NECESSARY COLUMN

When my daughter was two years old, my son was born with congenital hypothyroidism. He started taking medicine at five days of age, and his tiny body had a rough time adjusting. Toss in food allergies and colic, and he cried for eight-hour stretches, napping for only ten minutes. Neither of us slept. I was losing it.

Finally, when Ethan was four months old, I told Rob I needed to hire a babysitter for two mornings a week so that I could leave the house. "We either pay for a sitter or for therapy for me," I told him, and I was dead serious.

A babysitter was cheaper.

At that time, I thought I would never write another published word. We hired childcare not so I could work for pay again, but because I needed to work at reclaiming wholeness—which is priceless.

Do you need to reclaim wholeness, too?

Friends, this is not a selfish thing to do. We care for so many other things, we must take care of ourselves, as well.

It's a lesson Erin, my dear friend from college, learned the hard way. Working full time while adjusting to parenthood left her feeling as though she underperformed in all areas of life. Wracked with guilt, she struggled to lower her expectations of herself. Erin's physical, emotional, and spiritual health suffered. Her journal entry here is telling:

> Baby steps toward finding myself & my motivation again . . . joined a gym, took 2 classes, actually rested, starting this journal, started taking my blood sugar [to see if gestational diabetes had gone away]—it only took until my daughter was 22 months to start remembering that I still exist & matter!
>
> I so love being Rachel's mama, but I am worried she is not going to have a mama left if all I do is work & take care of her.

Soon after she wrote that, Erin learned from the doctor that she was, in fact, prediabetic. "At least getting the diagnosis has now moved caring for myself into the 'necessary column' where it needed to be all along," she told me. After several weeks of exercising, eating right, and making rest a priority, she finally felt "like there is hope and that this is indeed a time-limited phase!"

Colleen, who has cared for her war-injured husband for more than a dozen years, makes sure to carve out time for herself. "I wither away and die if I do not," she told me, "and you cannot care for others when you are not caring for yourself. To be the best wife, caregiver, mother, grandmother, and mentor, I *must* be recharged as well." In addition to her morning routine of coffee, devotions, and prayer, she does something creative at least once a week.

We best care for ourselves not when we ignore our stress, but when we acknowledge it and respond in healthy ways. When Brené Brown interviewed people she considered "wholehearted," she discovered that they "weren't anxiety-free or even anxiety-averse; they were anxiety aware. They were committed to a way of living where anxiety was a reality but not a lifestyle."[11]

What a relief to understand that we don't have to be stress-free to be whole! Stressful situations happen all the time. Even positive stresses—things like a wedding, a new house, a new job—are still forms of stress. When we are aware of how they affect us, we can better respond.

Maria, whose daughter has Angelman syndrome, says her husband tries to give her time alone to recharge. "What works for me is getting at least two hours alone where I can be outside or in a place outside my normal routines and read, listen to music, talk to Jesus, journal," she told me. "This clears my head and helps me regain perspective.

Ideally, my husband and I will find a way to give each other two hours like this every week. But we have to fight really hard for something like that."

Maria is also more aware of her own warning signs that signal a meltdown may be on the horizon. "I get grouchy, easily frustrated, and overly perfectionistic about trivial things. I am learning to try to pause and just stop, take a break and reset. If I've started taking it out on my husband, I just tell him what's happening and apologize."

It's time to place caring for yourself in the "necessary column," as Erin put it. Don't wait until you reach a crisis point to make your well-being a priority.

BREAK IT UP

Picture in your mind a calendar jammed with activities and appointments that fill every square. There's no breathing room there—unless you schedule some. It's time to break things up with a little white space. Whether once a week, twice a month, or whenever you can, claim some time for yourself to recharge. Schedule it and treat it as time that is spoken for, rather than a slot to be filled in if some activity or event pops up. Reclaiming yourself *is* the event.

On Thursdays, my friend Annabel has a "night off." She leaves the house at seven o'clock while her husband puts their sons to bed. "I can do whatever I want," she says. "It's my time to have a break and it's pretty important to me." Annabel and her husband also take turns staying with the kids while the other spouse has a night out with friends. "I have realized how good that is for me as an extrovert," she told me. "Those times out with other people give me energy."

Charlotte, my friend who is a doctor, uses vacation time from work on the occasional weekday, taking her kids to preschool and spending the rest of the time on herself. "I use the day to do whatever lingering errands I need to do but also try to do something I usually don't do, like go shopping or get a facial," she told me. "I used to feel guilty about doing it, but it is really rejuvenating."

Another way to give yourself a break is to figure out what can be cut from your schedule completely or done in a less time-consuming way.

My friend Kristi, the counselor, loves to cook, but on evenings when she teaches class or attends sporting events, she orders takeout. "There's already enough complication between sitters, working, and differing schedules—I don't need that extra stress," she told me. "What I do rely on for stress management and emotional health is exercise. Going without it for a few days can lead me to feeling squeezed."

While caring for her mother, my friend Rosie was hospitalized four times in one year—and realized it was time to give herself a break. She shared with me, "Instead of trying to be 'Super Daughter,' I hired an LPN and housekeeper to help Mom at her senior apartment. I stopped taking her out each week to get her hair done, and had Mom order two wigs—I would just take the wigs in to be cleaned! When she was in the nursing home, we paid extra for the transportation van and attendant to bring her to my house." Rosie also asked out-of-town siblings for more help, and began scheduling quarterly trips or slumber parties with her three best friends—"Best idea ever!" she said. "I also spent more time in the Word to get stronger spiritually, and I went to counseling to take care of myself emotionally."

Kimberly Spragg sets an alarm that goes off many nights at 8:30 p.m. "That reminds me to stop using my cell phone for anything but receiving calls," she told me. "This helps me wind down, lets me focus on reading and time with God, and gets me off social media at night."

If you're not inspired enough already, take a look at the following list of other ways we can give ourselves some breathing room:

- Double or triple your cooking for a given meal, so you can eat one and freeze the rest for later days.
- Hire help with housework or enlist family members to clean with you . . . or just don't clean as much.
- Use grocery delivery if it's available in your area.
- Take advantage of apps and web sites that allow you to manage to-do lists, shop for clothing, or order household staples—each can save time and energy for more important things.
- Group errands into one day each week.
- If you have children, carefully consider the impact of each extracurricular activity on the family schedule before agreeing to participation.
- Minimize how often you reach for your smartphone. You don't need to respond to every beep and ping instantly—those interruptions can whittle away your time before you know it.
- Exercise. Even a few times a week helps the brain think more clearly and better cope with stress.
- Simplify holiday hustle. Limit the number of gifts you exchange, pare down your holiday menus

or use a catering service, carefully choose just a few special events or parties to attend, make and freeze holiday cookies weeks or months before you'll eat them. (Or skip the baking and *buy* whatever treats you want.)

- Cap the clutter. Throw out or donate what you're not using, wearing, or playing with. You'll spend less time digging through it, moving it around, and tripping over it.
- When you have a few minutes of waiting, such as for coffee to brew, don't automatically reach for your phone to scroll through your social media feeds—rather than filling your thoughts with your friends' news, take a moment to think, pray, and prepare yourself mentally for what's next on your agenda.
- Get up earlier.
- Go to bed earlier.
- If you can't get away for a few hours, snatch twenty to thirty minutes with a good book in a quiet corner.
- Get a professional massage. (You will love it!)

Look for ways to slow down, do less, and breathe more deeply.

A RHYTHM OF REST

In *Little House in the Big Woods* by Laura Ingalls Wilder, Pa tells a story: When Laura's Grandpa was a boy, Sabbath was strictly observed. After supper on Saturday, Grandpa's father read aloud from the Bible and prayed, and then the entire family went straight to bed with no playing, laughing, or talking.

Sunday morning, they ate a cold breakfast, since cooking was forbidden as work, then walked to church, since hitching the horses was forbidden work. They were to walk without talking, laughing, or even smiling. After church and another cold meal, the children were to sit on a bench and study their catechism until sundown.

One Sunday afternoon, desperate to try out the new sled they had finished building the day before, Grandpa and his two brothers snuck out of the house when their father fell asleep in his chair. Just one silent run down the hill outside their home, and they'd slip back inside—but they didn't plan on the large black pig in their path. The sled scooped up the pig, and the terrified animal squealed loudly the rest of the way down the hill. As they passed their house, the boys saw their father standing in the doorway, watching.

When the sun set, concluding Sabbath, the boys were taken to the woodshed for their punishment. As hilarious as I find the image of a squealing pig and three terrified, silent boys racing downhill on a sled, I can't help but cringe for these kids, too.

God gave the Sabbath to Israel as a special "sign" that they belonged to Him. "The Israelites are to observe the Sabbath, celebrating it for the generations to come as a lasting covenant. It will be a sign between me and the Israelites forever, for in six days the LORD made the heavens and the earth, and on the seventh day he rested and was refreshed" (Exodus 31:16–17). It was a day of rest and refreshment for man and beast.

But here's a truth which may have surprised Laura's great-grandpa. As Warren Wiersbe writes, "There is no evidence in Scripture that God ever gave the original Sabbath command to the Gentiles, or that it was repeated for the church to obey. Nine of the Ten Commandments are repeated in the church epistles, but the Sabbath commandment is not repeated. However, Paul makes it clear that believers must not make 'special days' a test of fellowship or spirituality."[12]

For support, Wiersbe refers to these two passages:

- "One person considers one day more sacred than another; another considers every day alike. Each of them should be fully convinced in their own mind" (Romans 14:5).
- "Therefore do not let anyone judge you by what you eat or drink, or with regard to a religious festival, a New Moon celebration or a Sabbath day. These are a shadow of the things that were to come; the reality, however, is found in Christ" (Colossians 2:16–17).

Still, there is great blessing in establishing a rhythm that includes rest. The more I've worked at keeping Sundays special, trusting God to handle my concerns while I release them, the more I've seen how He uses that day to refresh me and my family.

The way Christians observe a day of rest has changed drastically through generations. Many rest on Sunday, while others, like my friend Cynthia, make Saturdays off-limits to work. "It's a boundary that says, 'I'm more than my work,'" she says. Many of my friends in ministry take Mondays off after busy weekends at church.

When God first commanded His people to observe a Sabbath rest (Exodus 16:23), they'd just come from generations of Egyptian bondage—and work was all they knew. Suddenly, the Jews were free. Free to just *be*, rather than *do*. Free to rest. It was a radical, revolutionary concept at the time. It's no coincidence that in the books of the law, God most frequently describes himself as, "I am the LORD your God, who brought you out of Egypt." Sabbath was a weekly reminder of the people's liberation. They needed it.

In *Rhythms of Grace*, Kerri Weems expounds on this beautifully: "For slaves, all the rhythms of life are dictated by the master's will. The same is true for us—we are servants of whatever gets the first and best of our time. We might not think of ourselves as being in bondage, but is there anything that more clearly signifies freedom from the systems and values of this world than the ability to cease working and to rest? If we can't rest, if we won't rest, then are we truly free?"[13]

And yet, there is grace in this, too. As we look at the Gospels, we see that Pharisees routinely scolded Jesus for violating Sabbath law. On one Sabbath, the disciples picked heads of grain to eat, and later Jesus healed a man with a shriveled hand. Both times, the Pharisees cried out, in essence, "You can't do that today!" Jesus replied by reminding them that no one would leave a sheep in a pit on the Sabbath—and people were far more valuable than animals. "Therefore it is lawful to do good on the Sabbath" (Matthew 12:12).

In Luke 13, the Pharisees challenged Jesus for healing a crippled woman on the Sabbath, and again Jesus silenced them, calling them hypocrites. Another time, He healed a lame man and told him to take up his mat and walk. "The day on which this took place was a Sabbath, and so the Jewish leaders said to the man who had been healed, 'It is the Sabbath; the law forbids you to carry your mat'" (John 5:9–10). The Pharisees loved the law too much, but Jesus was—and still is—Lord of the Sabbath (Mark 2:28).

Kimberly Spragg reserves Sundays as a day when she uses her phone only for receiving calls. "I have to keep my phone on so students can reach me, but I can leave it face-down and keep it from distracting me," she told me. "While I do give myself some leeway in times of stress, I seek to keep Sunday a work-free day. That allows me to go home after church and read or nap, spend time with friends, and just putter around my house and prep for the week ahead."

My friend Dana shares what Sabbath rest looks like in her family today: "I find that to truly make a Sabbath work for me, I can't stay at home. I'm too tempted to tidy up, catch up, clean up . . . so it's best if we can go somewhere else. Maybe it's visiting our grandparents for the afternoon, or heading to the beach, or having a cookout at a nearby park. We try to make our Sabbath include connecting with community and enjoying nature whenever possible."

Your personal rhythm of rest will vary according to your season or stage of life, your health, the health of your family, and other factors. If you aren't in the habit of taking a regular break from the routine, ask God to show you what that could look like. When you're tempted to push through long periods of time without caring for yourself, remember: Neglecting the needs of *your* body and spirit is never the right solution. We are not slaves. We are free to lean, and free to rest. Give yourself a little more space, and breathe easy.

Rest from Stress

An emergency room nurse by day and a writer by night, Jordyn Redwood is busy. "Not just days upon days of a full agenda but balancing a myriad of tasks and responsibilities," she says. "A spouse. Children. Aging parents. Stressful jobs. And downtime is used to catch up on life—housecleaning, doing laundry, and maybe squeezing in a volunteer activity or hosting a play date to try and ease the guilt of how I'm burning the candle at both ends."

Over several months, staff turnover in her emergency department meant a decline in the overall experience level of the nursing staff, putting increased pressure on veteran nurses like Jordyn. While it was once rare for a patient to die in her department, now they had lost several. The combined stress took a toll on everyone.

"You could just see it in my coworkers' eyes, and in mine, after a shift," she says. "Bone weary tiredness. But nurses are a proud bunch. We put ourselves in stressful—even risky—situations to care for you and your loved ones, but when it comes to us we're the last on the list. We consider it a badge of honor, almost, to not need anyone else. If our patient dies and we turn around and take the next critical patient without batting an eye, then we're strong. We're still standing. We're resilient."

What she's learned, however, is just the opposite. "Standing up after a crisis—just pushing forward—is not resiliency. It's merely survival."

When staff morale became a concern for her unit's management team, they invited a hospital chaplain to address them. One thing he shared was that resiliency is connected to passion. "We have to dedicate time to what makes us passionate, in order to come through periods of stress better," says Jordyn. "For me, though I love writing and sharing my stories, I am passionate about needle-work. I know, crazy, right? Truly, it is the one thing that relaxes me—where I don't have any extra expectations from others."

The chaplain pointed out that after a strenuous physical event—like an exercise class or a 5K race—rest is expected. "When people overexert themselves physically we kind of shake our fingers at them and say, 'Well no wonder you're sick, you didn't take time to rest,'" Jordyn says. "But we're not very good at this when crushing emotional things happen. We're expected to stand up, brush the dirt off, and go on. In nursing, this happens every day across the country. We need rest from emotional stress just as much as from physical stress. People need to take care of themselves in the best way for them."

A true introvert, Jordyn needs time alone to rejuvenate. For a few years, she'd been telling her husband she needed a weekend by herself. "So when I was offered a posh cabin by a lake in Minnesota for a week, very inexpensively, I basically said 'I'm going'—for my sanity."

More than one person called her decision selfish. "I found this interesting because my husband takes a men's ski trip every year and these comments aren't ever made to him," she says. "Women have been expected always to serve others, while doing self-care is seen as greedy. I couldn't help but think to myself, *This is why so many women have nervous breakdowns.*"

Despite the criticism, Jordyn took that trip to the cabin, finally taking care of herself. "That trip to the cabin was just what I needed for rest," she told me. "The time alone helped me think through a critical life decision and come home more centered and focused."

Your Turn

1. Are the things that keep you busy energizing you, or are you burning out?
2. In what areas could you do a better job of respecting your body's needs?
3. What is one practical thing you can do this week to work toward that goal?
4. What are your warning signs that you aren't taking care of yourself? What can you do as soon as you notice them?
5. Do you need to cut something out of your schedule to preserve some time for your own care? What could that be?

Truths to Trust

Neglecting the needs of your body and spirit
is never the right solution.
We are free to lean, and free to rest.

CHAPTER 9

Prayerful Vision

Many are the plans in a person's heart,
but it is the LORD's purpose that prevails.

PROVERBS 19:21

Be Thou my Vision, O Lord of my heart;
Naught be all else to me, save that Thou art.

OLD IRISH HYMN,
ENGLISH LYRICS BY ELEANOR HULL

Before I write a novel, I take a giant bulletin board and cover it with images that help me see the world I'm trying to create. I pin pictures of natural settings, architecture and floor plans, maps of cities and surrounding areas. I show my characters in period fashions, and if I have fabric swatches to represent what they wear—wool, silk, linen—I'll add those as well. Then I plot the course of the main characters' lives on index cards and post those on my office wall. It's all very messy, but seeing how the places and characters and events fit together gives me a vision for the story. I can then write the book.

So I understand the concept behind creating "vision boards" for our own lives. Many people find it useful as inspiration to pin pictures or words on some type of bulletin board. Vision boarders say that if you think about your dreams hard enough and long enough, they are bound to happen—either because you're sending the right vibe into the universe (*ahem*), or because you'll naturally take steps to achieve your goals when you're reminded of them daily.

Now, I'm all for setting goals and posting reminders, and visual inspiration is plenty of fun. But while shaping a novel is one thing, plotting my *life* is something else entirely. I make the best decisions I can with the information I have at the time, but I don't see all the pieces and how they fit together. Nor could I ever choose every one of them. But God does. He is the Author of my story. If my vision for life doesn't match His, all the visualizing in the world isn't going to make my version happen: "Many are the plans in a person's heart, but it is the LORD's purpose that prevails" (Proverbs 19:21).

Without prayer and the guidance of the Holy Spirit, I may pick the wrong goals and measures of success. If I focus on the wrong priorities, I'll feel frustrated and defeated when I fail to achieve those things. Worse than that, I'll miss out on what God really had in mind.

But when we do pray and invite God to direct our plans for today and for our tomorrows, though the road may not always be smooth, we can trust Him to make our paths straight (Proverbs 3:5–6). He will lead us directly where He wants us.

VISION CHECK

It's not always easy to discern God's plan at every stage of life. But fixing our gaze on Jesus is always in season. "And let us run with perseverance the race marked out for us, fixing our eyes on Jesus, the pioneer and perfecter of faith" (Hebrews 12:1–2). Whatever we may perceive our God-given purpose to be, keeping the Lord uppermost in our affections will make it far easier to follow His leading.

When my friend Bettina and her husband, Rob, became empty nesters, they cherished the memories from their child-rearing years and enjoyed rich, healthy relationships with their adult children. "It became very apparent that this new season only held two choices for us—soak up all of those blessings for ourselves and become fat on them, or pour those blessings back into the world, sharing the love we had been privileged to receive," Bettina said.

They prayed about how that "pouring out" might look, and the answer took time to develop. "We continued to do the things in front of us each day while we asked God to show us what this new season had for us in the way of service," Bettina told me.

One closed door and the encouragement of a godly friend set Bettina and Rob on the path of foster parenting. "Strangely enough," she said, "at no point in the application and approval process, which ended up being a very long three years for us, were we ever completely convinced that we were going to actually become foster parents. We just kept taking the next step that we felt had been placed in front of us—and praying for wisdom. It was only when they placed that first precious baby in our arms that we realized we had found the place God had for us in this new season."

Prayer was key for Bettina and Rob as they sought to obey God's leading.

BLIND SPOTS

As we each seek God's vision in our lives, let's be aware of our potential blind spots.

BLIND SPOT #1: ADOPTING A VISION FOR YOUR LIFE OR SEASON FROM ANYONE OTHER THAN GOD.

Plenty of people will give their opinions on what you should or should not do with your life. Bettina and Rob could have listened to those who suggested they were past the appropriate age for fostering children. Instead, they chose to listen to God.

I sometimes wonder about the adulterous woman Jesus saved from death by stoning (John 8:1–11). After He lavished grace upon her and told her to leave her life of sin, what did she do? Where did she go, and who did she tell of her miraculous escape from the mob? The Bible is silent on these questions, but it seems likely that at least some people in the woman's life would have voiced doubt as to whether she could follow through in obedience to Jesus's command. They may have called her "sinner," but Jesus called her to be holy.

Likewise, the disciple Matthew likely heard his fair share of mocking whispers, at least at first. Tax collectors like him were despised for their dishonesty and corruption. Could a man like that really become a follower of Jesus? People may have called Matthew "sinner," but Jesus called him to follow—and Matthew did.

Have others cast doubt on your calling, too? Whatever they've said, whatever label they have put on you or your life, God's call is stronger.

"I've had a few people tell me that I work too much," shares Kimberly Spragg. "I used to feel really guilty about it, until an older mentor—a senior member of a university—told me that my ability to work like I do is a gift and that I shouldn't feel bad about it. Of course we all need rest, but we all have different capabilities. I am single and I have the time to work like this for the time being. That's not a bad thing—it's a gift!"

Godly counsel, such as Kimberly received, will resonate with whatever the Holy Spirit is also telling you. God's voice is the One that matters most.

BLIND SPOT #2: COMPARING GOD'S CALLING FOR YOU WITH HIS CALLING FOR ANYONE ELSE.

When we're unsure of how (or if) God is leading us, it's especially tempting to look at someone else's fruitful life and want to pattern our own after it, hoping to achieve similar success or praise. Don't give in. God's blueprint for your life is unique. God's timing and His purposes are for you alone.

Julie Lessman has a good friend with six kids and a dozen or so grandchildren, a woman who runs a day-care in her home, breeds dogs, grows and sells vegetables, maintains a sideline bakery business, takes food to shut-ins and cancer patients . . . and still manages to write about four novels a year. "In the beginning," Julie told me, "I sensed her mind-set to be that whatever she accomplished, we could, too, if we just pulled up our 'big-girl panties' and got busy." The idea bothered Julie, because even though she was considered "a shaker and a mover" by friends and family, "I could not only *not* keep up with her, but I couldn't keep up with all *I* had to do either. I am happy to say that my friend's amazing productivity no longer bothers me, because God has shown me that she has been gifted with an abundance of stamina and energy that most people do not have. So I have learned to let it go and admire her for all she gets done."

Don't measure your story against anyone else's. Think about what God is revealing to *you*, rather than what He gives others.

Comparing our positions in God's kingdom is a pit-fall that has been around since Jesus walked the earth. His disciples were eager to know who was the greatest in the kingdom of heaven (Matthew 18:1). It's obvious from Paul's letters to Corinth that the early church struggled with this, too (1 Corinthians 12:15–20). Rest in the assurance that, as Susie Larson wrote, "As Christ followers, we are not too small for big things, and not too big for small things."[1]

BLIND SPOT #3: STRETCHING A SHORT-TERM ASSIGNMENT INTO A LONG-TERM COMMITMENT.

Several years ago, our church suffered from a lack of Sunday school teachers. Week after week, the same call for volunteers was printed in the bulletin, and the same plea issued from the pulpit. Finally one morning, in exasperation, our pastor blurted out, "This is not a lifetime commitment! You don't have to teach until Jesus comes back!"

Most of us laughed, I think, because there is an unspoken assumption that when one signs up for a ministry, it could go on indefinitely. But hear this: just because God leads you to a position doesn't mean it's forever. Just because He leads you to a particular place doesn't mean you'll never move again. Just because He brings a person into your life doesn't mean you're destined to marry him. Our seasons change, sometimes in unexpected ways.

Jesus's official ministry on earth lasted only three years. He did not heal all the sick people, feed all the hungry, or bless all the poor. He traveled some, preaching and teaching, but not nearly as far as the apostles would go. Yet right before He was crucified, Jesus prayed, "I have brought you glory on earth by finishing the work you gave me to do" (John 17:4). While some were waiting for Jesus to overthrow Roman rule, He declared His work already done!

In the same way, the assignments God gives us may be for the short term rather than the long. Be alert to the possibility that God's vision for your life may include a sharp turn to a different path.

BLIND SPOT #4: TRYING TO FORCE A LONG-TERM VISION AHEAD OF ITS TIME.

We live in a culture that doesn't like to wait, but in God's kingdom, we often find ourselves in what can feel like a holding pattern. We may sense strongly that God wants to use us in a certain way, but the daily demands of the current season prevent us from pursuing that. As difficult as it can be to wait, trust that God's perfect timing will prevail. If God has given you a vision of the future, don't try to force its fulfillment early.

In Genesis 15, we read that God promised Abram his descendants would be as numerous as the stars—which meant that Sarai would need to bear a son. When that didn't come to pass on her preferred schedule, Sarai was so desperate to fulfill the vision that she urged Abram to sleep with her slave Hagar. He did, and once Hagar became pregnant, Sarai's jealousy and bitterness grew into mistreatment of her slave. Sarai had tried to force God's vision for her family ahead of His timing.

In Isaiah 64:4, the prophet names God the One "who acts on behalf of those who wait for him." When we wait on God, we can rest assured that He is working. But we shouldn't just twiddle our thumbs. What may seem like unrelated small assignments in the meantime may actually be part of our preparation for later. Ours should be an active waiting while God matures us for what He has planned.

Nichole Nordeman, whose story you read at the end of Chapter 4, says, "God was so generous to continue to give me creative opportunities while I was home during that season where I wasn't recording and I wasn't touring, I wasn't traveling." After almost ten years in the active waiting mode, the decision to record and perform again "just felt right."[2]

We've all spent time waiting, haven't we? Perhaps it was for a child to join your family through birth, foster care, or adoption. Maybe you're waiting for a job to come through, or for medical test results. To "wait on the Lord" as it is most often used in the Bible, means to "hope, expect, look eagerly." Throughout the Psalms, we're urged to do just that (see Psalms 27:14; 33:20; 37:7). Then in Isaiah, we get a promise worth clinging to: "Yet those who wait for the LORD will gain new strength; they will mount up with wings like eagles; they will run and not get tired; they will walk and not become weary" (Isaiah 40:31 NASB).

As you wait for God's long-term vision to come to pass, wait on the Lord and renew your strength. Some day you may look back and see that after a period of waiting, your position and preparation have aligned "for such a time as this" (Esther 4:14).

BLIND SPOT #5: PLACING THE VISION ABOVE GOD.

Following God means following the path He opens up for us. We grow passionate about what we feel called to do. The danger, of course, is the possibility of falling more in love with God's plan for you than you are with God himself.

After Abram and Sarai—renamed by God as Abraham and Sarah—finally had their long-promised son, Isaac, God asked the unthinkable: that Abraham sacrifice the boy's life. Look at how God phrases this command: "Take *your son, your only son, whom you love—Isaac—*and go to the region of Moriah. Sacrifice him there as a burnt offering on a mountain I will show you" (Genesis 22:2, italics mine). As if Abraham needed any reminding about how special Isaac was, God really laid it out there, didn't He? Isaac wasn't just a beloved son—he was the only fulfillment of the Abrahamic covenant.

Sacrificing Isaac was the ultimate test of faith, and Abraham passed. He bound Isaac, placed him on an altar, and raised a knife to kill him. But at the last possible moment, God stopped Abraham from harming the boy, saying, "Now I know that you fear God, because you have not withheld from me your son, your only son" (v. 12).

Friends, sometimes God asks *us* to lay the vision He gave us on the altar. Sometimes He blesses us just for being willing to let it go—and sometimes He really does want us to sacrifice what we hold most dear.

In his book *Me, Myself, and Bob,* VeggieTales creator Phil Vischer candidly shares how he intended Bob and Larry and the gang to become big enough to rival Disney. He envisioned a theme park that would point kids to scriptural truth, courtesy of winsome talking vegetables. A series of business relationships and management decisions culminated in a lawsuit that went against his Big Idea Productions, causing Vischer to lose control of the company and its characters. Though the lawsuit was later overturned, Vischer's dream had died—and died hard.

At the end of his book, Phil Vischer unpacked lessons relevant for all of us. "Why would God want us to let go of our dreams?" he asks. "Because *anything* I am unwilling to let go of is an idol, and I am in sin."[3] And it is sin to prefer a dream to God, even when that dream does great things. Vischer's total preoccupation with his own dreams and ideas, he wrote, "rendered me virtually useless to the people around me. Useless. I was failing to demonstrate God's love. I was failing to walk with God."[4] When he realized this painful truth, he fell to his knees and begged for God's forgiveness.

In 2005, Vischer started a new company called Jellyfish, which would eventually birth the *What's in the Bible?* DVDs my family loves. The company was so named because jellyfish can't choose their own course, but have to float with the current. "For a jellyfish, long-range planning is an act of extreme hubris," Vischer writes. He explains:

> And so it is for me. I believed I could change the world, and the weight of that belief almost crushed me. But guess what—apart from God, I can do nothing. I can't get anywhere. . . . My ability to accomplish anything good is dependent on my willingness to dwell in the current of God's will. To wait on God and let him supply my form and my direction. Like a jellyfish. . . .
>
> So our plan at Jellyfish—and it's an odd one, I'll admit—is to make no long-range plans unless God gives them explicitly . . . no inspiring Power-Point vision statements. Just a group of people on their knees, trusting God for guidance each day. Holding everything loosely but God himself.[5]

PUTTING SUCCESS IN PERSPECTIVE

As you pray for God's guidance for your life, both in the short term and the long term, ask Him how to measure how well you're carrying out His plan for you. As Phil Vischer learned all too well, the important thing is not to achieve fame and notoriety in the world's eyes, but to please the One who gave us all our gifts and capacities. It's helpful to ask yourself:

- How will I define success in what God is calling me to do?
- What will my obedience in this area look like?
- What will give me confirmation that I'm on the right track?
- What sort of thing would cause me to put on the brakes and reevaluate how my life is matching up to God's plan for me?
- Who is a trusted, godly person that could mentor me?

We are called to obedience and faithfulness, and to trust God. Our lives will bear fruit when we abide in Him while pursuing our purpose. That doesn't necessarily always lead to success as the world sees it.

Then again, it just might. Success is not a sin, and it isn't sinful to want to be great at what we do, from child-rearing to blogging to corporate managing. Striving for excellence is a good thing: "So whether you eat or drink or whatever you do, do it all for the glory of God" (1 Corinthians 10:31). Paul also tells us to run the race as though to win the prize (1 Corinthians 9:24). I'm pretty sure he's not referring to a participation trophy here! Doing our best brings glory to God.

And yet, success can also carry its own dangers, mostly related to pride. To combat Satan's lies in this area, remember:

* Achievement is by God's grace.
* Achievement is possible thanks to all those who invested in us along the way.
* We are no more worthy of God's love after success than we ever were before it.
* We are no less in need of a Savior after success than we ever were before.
* We are no more important than those who have tried and "failed."
* Achievement is not more valuable than the One who allowed us to succeed.
* Achievement does not mean it's time to "retire" from striving for excellence.
* Success provides a platform to glorify God, not ourselves.
* Success on a large stage does not mean we can forsake the daily call to be humble and Christlike to others.

As we contemplate what success may look like in our lives, remember, Phil Vischer says, "God is enough. Just God. And he isn't 'enough' because he can make our dreams come true—no, you've got him confused with Santa or Merlin or Oprah. The God who created the universe is enough for us—even without our dreams."[6]

Looking back over her last year and the changes it brought at home and work, Krista says, "It has become so clear that running so hard after the things of this world can be fun and somewhat fulfilling because we have gifts and abilities in these areas, but deeply relying on God is what life is all about—relying on God, and trying to see the plans He has for us." She continues:

> The plans He has for our lives are deeper and richer than anything we're hungry for. There are so many distractions that get in the way. Things that are good but not great. If you can get to the point where you allow yourself a break, and really want God's best, you can have a life that is full but not always terribly busy. There is no prize at the end of the day for the one who does the most tasks or who is the busiest. It's the day-to-day trying to live a life of honoring Christ, and allowing Him to live through us.

WHEN YOU JUST CAN'T SEE

Sometimes, though, we can barely get through the day, let alone look ahead to the future. It might be that the daily demands, or grief, or family crises, or emotional turmoil are just so intense, they eclipse everything else. I can relate to that.

My struggle with depression took place more than fifteen years ago, but I still remember vividly how stuck I was, mentally. I was drowning in the "right now," with no thought that the next moment might be any different or that anything could possibly change. The despair that had enveloped me was so dark, I could not see my own hand in front of my face. Without vision, there's not much hope. It's very hard to get anywhere when you can't see.

If you're in a similar situation right now, listen to this: "Who among you fears the LORD and obeys the word of his servant? Let the one who walks in the dark, who has no light, trust in the name of the LORD and rely on their God" (Isaiah 50:10).

Even when we can't see much from our point of view, God sees it all. He sees the big picture, the long view of things, just like Jesus did with Mary and Martha. He had decided against healing their brother, Lazarus, not because He was careless or mean but because He knew God would get greater glory if He raised Lazarus from the dead instead (John 11).

Oh, how we long to know what God sees that we can't! But if we could see everything at once, we wouldn't have to trust Him. God wants to use the hard times of our lives to build our relationship with Him. In our darkest hours, what we believe about God's character can sustain us. Do we believe that He is sovereign and in control? Do we believe that He is trustworthy? Our answers to these questions are more important than knowing what tomorrow will hold. I love what Carolyn Custis James says here:

> God's character is crucial, for there are moments in life when God's goodness and love seem to come under a blackout. No matter how we strain our eyes, we cannot see any good, not a trace of God's love. . . . When faith cannot find something tangible to grasp, we are compelled to fly back to the ark of God's unchanging, unfailing character. But faith will not find much of a foothold here if God is a stranger to us. Faith, in the final analysis, is trusting

someone you know, even when you don't always un-derstand what he is doing.[7]

When you feel lost in the dark and you don't see a way out, remember this: God doesn't just see His path for you. He also sees *you*. Maybe you don't see the way out. But you aren't lost.

Earlier in this chapter, we spent some time discussing Abraham, Sarah, and Isaac. But God's conversation with Hagar, the slave Sarah mistreated, should not be missed. After she fled, pregnant and alone, the angel of God met her in the wilderness. He came to Hagar right where she was, in middle of her mess, and He called her *by name* in Genesis 16:8—"Hagar, slave of Sarai, where have you come from, and where are you going?" (By the way, I can think of no better questions to ponder in a chapter about prayerful vision!) After they spoke, Hagar named *God*, calling Him El Roi, "the God who sees me" (Genesis 16:13).

Hagar was unwanted and unloved. Used and cast aside. Yet she was not invisible to God, and neither are you. As you prayerfully seek God's vision for your life, remember that *El Roi*, "the God who sees me," is also the God who sees you.

SEEING THE INVISIBLE

So far, we've talked about vision mostly in terms of fixing our eyes on Jesus and looking ahead to the future. But there's another kind of vision that warrants our attention here, too. Though we may not "see" it, there is a spiritual battle going on right now. "Be alert and of sober mind. Your enemy the devil prowls around like a roaring lion looking for someone to devour" (1 Peter 5:8).

When we lean into our God-given purposes, we're growing His kingdom—which means we are a threat to Satan's kingdom of darkness. The fact that we can't see the arrows he flings our way—discouragement, doubt, insecurity, jealousy, despair, bitterness—makes them no less real. Any of these could sabotage our effectiveness and our capacity to produce fruit. But God never leaves us to fend for ourselves.

Finally, be strong in the Lord and in his mighty power. Put on the full armor of God, so that you can take your stand against the devil's schemes. For our struggle is not against flesh and blood, but against the rulers, against the authorities, against the powers of this dark world and against the spiritual forces of evil in the heavenly realms. Therefore put on the full armor of God, so that when the day of evil comes, you may be able to stand your ground, and after you have done everything, to stand. Stand firm then, with the belt of truth buckled around your waist, with the breastplate of righteousness in place, and with your feet fitted with the readiness that comes from the gospel of peace. In addition to all this, take up the shield of faith, with which you can extinguish all the flaming arrows of the evil one. Take the helmet of salvation and the sword of the Spirit, which is the word of God.

EPHESIANS 6:10–17

As we arm ourselves spiritually, we are also told to pray and to be alert. I first shared the following five enemy tactics in my devotional book for military wives, *Faith*

Deployed . . . Again, but Satan uses these methods against all of us.[8]

1. **Satan tempts us with what seems attractive but ultimately harms us.** Nothing about the forbidden fruit looked harmful to Eve, making it easy for Satan to tempt her with it. Likewise, our temptations may come sugarcoated. A goal is wonderful until it becomes an idol. A friendship is dangerous when it influences us toward discontent.

2. **Satan plants doubt about or contradicts God's Word.** In the Garden of Eden, Satan questioned what God had said (Genesis 3:1). Then he told Eve God had lied to her. And the devil would love for *us* to doubt God's truth, too. *God can't really use you. Look what everyone else is doing. You're not good enough.* Whenever you hear those whispers of deception, don't trust them. Trust the Bible.

3. **Satan tries to twist Scripture for his purposes.** He misused Psalm 91:11–12 when he spoke to Jesus in the wilderness (Luke 4:9–10). If Satan can get us to claim only half a verse, such as "I can do all this" without "through him who gives me strength" (Philippians 4:13), he accomplishes his purpose. We must be vigilant about taking God's Word in context.

4. **Satan comes at us when we're most vulnerable.** Eve and Jesus were both alone when Satan tempted them. Don't allow yourself to be isolated from

other believers who can help bring perspective to your struggles. Most of us are also vulnerable when we're tired, stressed, or hurting. Be especially on guard during these times.

5. **Satan uses well-intentioned Christians.** This one is hard to swallow, but take a look at Matthew 16:21–23. Peter rebuked Jesus for predicting His own death, and Jesus called Peter "Satan"! Peter was likely shocked to hear that, but his words refuted God's will. As we already discussed in Chapter 4, we need to weigh all our counsel against the truth of Scripture, and listen for the resonance the Holy Spirit provides.

Armed for spiritual battle and alert to enemy tactics, we'll be far more equipped to follow God's marching orders. As we consider our day, our season, and our future, may we prayerfully seek the vision He has written over our lives. Though we may not always feel like it's true, His plan is far better than anything we can devise on our own.

A Vision to Thrive

Joanna Gaines could have throttled her husband, Chip.

Before they were stars of the hit HGTV show *Fixer Upper*, they were raising their four kids and developing properties in Waco, Texas, while flipping the houses they lived in. But when Chip announced he'd sold their stately home in Castle Heights, Joanna was the one who flipped.

"This is a *forever* house," she told him.[9]

He disagreed. It was a nice house, but it was still inventory. Chip drove Joanna to the house he'd already bought for them to live in next. It was a long, gray, one-story shotgun house without character, charm, or style. She hated it.

But by now, she'd learned to quickly adjust her thinking while she caught up to Chip's vision.

The Castle Heights home they had just sold was beautiful—so beautiful that it felt like more of a showplace than a family home. Maybe this ugly, shotgun house would be different. Maybe God was leading them here for a reason, just as He'd been leading the Gaines family in surprising ways all along.

In their first year of marriage, Joanna opened a successful home décor boutique. But when she was pregnant with her second baby, she sensed God telling her it was time to close shop and stay home with her kids.

"I kept asking God, 'Are you sure this is the right move? If it is, why does it seem so painful and hard?' That's when I heard that gentle whisper, *Joanna, if you trust me with your dreams, I'll take them further than you could have ever imagined.*

It is no easy thing to trust in God, to walk away from a career, to give it all up not knowing if you can ever get it back or even come close. But I did it. I heeded his voice, and somehow I found peace about it."[10]

Time and time again, God's vision for Joanna's family proved to be even greater than her original plan.

When she and Chip brought their kids to that shotgun house, they immediately began running down the hallway and sliding in their socks. Joanna thought, "My kids love it in here. They can be kids. I'm going to design around that."[11]

It was a turning point for her as a designer and a mom. "I came to a brand-new conclusion: 'If all I'm doing is creating beautiful spaces, I'm failing. But if I'm creating beautiful spaces where families are thriving, then I'm really doing something.' Doing that became my new calling."[12]

Joanna realized her quest for perfection was pointless. "Nothing was ever going to be perfect the way I had envisioned it in the past. Did I want to keep spending my energy on that effort, or did I want to step out of that obsession and to enjoy my kids, maybe allowing myself to get messy right along with them in the process? I chose the latter—and that made all the difference."[13]

When Joanna and her family moved into their new house, designed with spaces to create and play, she saw everyone come alive in ways she'd never seen before.

Since then, the Gaines family survived a financial crisis within their development company when an economic downturn caused the bank to slash their line of credit;

moved to a farm they love; became the stars of *Fixer Upper*; and reopened Joanna's shop—only on a much larger scale (to the tune of sixteen thousand square feet) in a new location.

"Not even a decade after I made that difficult decision to close my shop to stay home with my babies, God delivered on the promise of making my dreams come true in ways that were bigger than I ever imagined," Joanna said.[14]

If there's anything Chip and Joanna want others to learn from their story, it's that "there's contentment in the journey. . . . And in times of doubt or times of joy, listen for that still, small voice. Know that God has been there from the beginning—and he will be there until . . . The End."[15]

Your Turn

1. Which of the five blind spots have you found yourself susceptible to? What happened?
2. Have others tried to force their own vision onto your life? How did you respond?
3. Have you experienced a season of waiting? If so, what value did you ultimately realize which you may not have seen at the time?
4. Are you willing to let go of your dream if God asks you to?

5. How have you noticed Satan attempting to use one or more of the "enemy tactics" on you? How can you arm yourself for the next time?

Truths to Trust

God loves to guide us when we ask Him.
God's vision for your life can be trusted.

CHAPTER 10

Amazing Grace

But he said to me, "My grace is sufficient for you, for my power is made perfect in weakness." Therefore I will boast all the more gladly about my weaknesses, so that Christ's power may rest on me.

2 CORINTHIANS 12:9

Under the yoke of grace, I rest content with where I am right here, right now, weaknesses and all—as long as I am walking close to Jesus.

KERRI WEEMS
Rhythms of Grace: Discovering God's Tempo for Your Life

2:30 *a.m.* The time glowed red in the dark. I quickly did the math. *I haven't been sleeping for five hours yet. I need more rest*, I told myself. All the sleep research I shared in Chapter 8 swirled through my mind. I'd done everything right last night—took a shower, read a book, prayed. I should have been sound asleep. *Hurry up!* I thought. *Go back to sleep before the adrenaline kicks in! You'll be a mess if you don't, you'll eat too much and start a pattern that may lead to diabetes! You won't be a good mom today, and you won't think clearly enough to write, and your book is due in six days!* My heart raced with the urgency of calming down.

I tried to wrestle myself back to sleep for an hour, before I gave up. Defeated, I tiptoed out of the room, grabbed my Bible, and started the day. After my (very) quiet time with God, I worked until I fell asleep on the sofa in my office around five.

When I finally got up again, it was after eight. Rob had already gone to work and I had missed giving my son his thyroid medicine at six. He has to wait two hours between medication and breakfast, so he was none too pleased with me.

I was none too pleased with myself, putting it mildly. By this time the day before, I had already picked up my daughter from her orchestra rehearsal and was helping both kids with their math. Today I was stiff, exhausted, behind . . . and beyond frustrated with myself.

Later in the morning, Rob messaged me, suggesting we go out for dinner to help make up for my less-than-stellar start to the day. It's "free pie day" at Village Inn, he pointed out.

Now, I love pie. But I told Rob we'd have to wait and see. "I feel like I have to earn it," I replied. *I don't deserve that*, I was thinking. *Let's see if I can redeem this day, and then maybe. If I'm not productive, it's leftovers or cereal again.*

Then I got back to work. On this chapter. On grace. Even as I did, I noticed some pain I'd had earlier in the week—in my right wrist, forearm, and elbow—had disappeared. I'd asked for prayer for that the day before, and now I was typing pain-free. Then this thought occurred to me: *Maybe it just means I haven't been working hard enough today.*

Oh, friends—I need this book as much as anyone else.

I know all about grace. Borrowing a definition from Kerri Weems, "Grace is God's undeserved favor that puts us in right relationship with Him, and grace is the power God gives that enables us to live the life He's called us to."[1] That means I can't *earn* God's favor. I already have it. It also means God gives me the power to live the life *He's* called me to—which may be different from the life I think I should be living.

I still struggle with feeling a need to earn my worth. I used to be even worse in this area, seething with self-loathing when I went to bed with unfinished work, and full of dread when I awoke the next day because I was convinced I'd fail yet again. I would just lie there, staring at the ceiling, unwilling to start another day because I couldn't bear any more proof of my own inadequacy.

This has been a vicious battle of the mind and spirit. Remember those enemy tactics from the end of Chapter 9? Satan used all five on me, and it took me far too long to realize what he was up to.

When I find ice cream melting in the refrigerator, I know Rob—sleep-deprived and not thinking clearly—put it there instead of the freezer. I give him grace. When my kids tried to help prepare sandbags and found the work too heavy, I didn't scold them for being weak. I applauded their efforts while shouldering the brunt of the work myself. Isn't that what our gracious God does for us all the time?

Yet if I don't produce to a certain standard in a given day, grace for myself is suddenly in very short supply. Shame comes knocking.

And shame is a bully. Why do we ever let him in, when it means evicting Grace?

Let's get this right, friends. Let's lean into God's grace for us, and give grace to ourselves.

GRACE UPON GRACE

One of the most often-quoted verses in the Christian faith (and rightly so) is Ephesians 2:8–9: "For it is by grace you have been saved, through faith—and this is not from yourselves, it is the gift of God—not by works, so that no one can boast." Works don't make us worthy of being saved. We can't earn salvation. If we could, that wouldn't be grace at all, but some kind of transaction. Grace is a gift. A gift that saves.

But that's not all grace does. Yes, it brings unbelievers into the fold, but grace also sustains those of us who have believed in Jesus. Listen to this: "Out of his fullness we have all received grace in place of grace already given. For the law was given through Moses; grace and truth came through Jesus Christ" (John 1:16–17). *Grace in place of grace already given.* The English Standard Version and the New American Standard Bible use the phrase "grace upon grace." That means God is still gifting us with what we don't deserve— His love, His peace, His strength.

In Paul's letter to the Corinthians, he writes of a thorn in his flesh. Theologians debate what the thorn may have been, but we know it was a burden and it was painful, either physically or emotionally. It could have been a drain on Paul's strength, minimizing his capacity to spread the gospel. But Paul reported that God told him, "My grace is sufficient for you, for my power is made perfect in weakness." So, Paul said, "I will boast all the more gladly about my weaknesses, so that Christ's power may rest on me" (2 Corinthians 12:9).

Grace sustains us. Not our own strength, nor our own power, lest any of us could boast.

When we look at how Paul opens and closes his letters to the early Christians, we notice a striking pattern:

- "Grace and peace to you from God our Father and the Lord Jesus Christ" (1 Corinthians 1:3).
- "The grace of the Lord Jesus be with you" (1 Corinthians 16:23).
- "Grace and peace to you from God our Father and the Lord Jesus Christ" (2 Corinthians 1:2).
- "May the grace of the Lord Jesus Christ, and the love of God, and the fellowship of the Holy Spirit be with you all" (2 Corinthians 13:14).

The pattern continues through the rest of the Pauline epistles. Every letter begins and ends with grace.

Everything begins and ends with grace. Let that one sink in for a moment. We are saved into relationship with Christ because of grace. We continue living in the fullness of His love because of grace. When our time on earth is done, grace will lead us all the way home.

Did you notice in the verses above that grace is often paired with peace? The connection stands to reason.

Certainly, if there is no grace, there is no peace. And if we do accept grace, we also have peace. "But now in Christ Jesus you who once were far away have been brought near by the blood of Christ. For he himself is our peace" (Ephesians 2:13–14).

Don't you love that? We have been brought near to Christ by His death and resurrection, which is the gift of grace. For He himself is our peace.

Grace means it's not about what *we* can do, but what *Christ* has already done for us.

Grace means we don't have to earn His love, strength, or power. He has already declared us worthy of these gifts—and it has nothing to do with our striving.

Grace means that when we fall short, all is not lost—because Jesus covers the distance between where we are and where we will someday be. "Therefore, there is now no condemnation for those who are in Christ Jesus, because through Christ Jesus the law of the Spirit who gives life has set you free from the law of sin and death" (Romans 8:1–2).

Grace means I'm going out to dinner with my family tonight no matter how far I get in my work.

We are free. Because of grace.

UNGRACIOUS MYTHS AND PEACE-GIVING TRUTHS

And yet, it's so easy to lose sight of grace amid all the details of our lives. Why? Let's take a look at just some of the ungracious myths that rob us of our peace.

Myth: If I'm not meeting my own expectations, I am less valuable.
Truth: Your value and worth have already been decided by the Creator of the universe. God so loved you that He gave His

one and only Son. He deems you worthy of an eternity in heaven with Him (John 3:16).

"I feel like I've fallen *so* short of my expectations for myself as a mother, writer, friend, and wife on more occasions than I'd like to count," shares Lisa. "God keeps reminding me that while much of this is a surprise to me, none of it is a surprise to Him. When I rest in that truth I feel His grace and am more peaceful about where I am. Our expectations for ourselves are often much more intense than God's expectations for us. And at other times, He has so much more for us than we could even imagine. Either way, we need to trust God and His plan and not be continually discouraged by the demise of our own plans."

Myth: If others disapprove of me or my decisions, I must have done something wrong.
Truth: Others' opinions of you do not affect your worth. Work with all your heart for the Lord, not for people (Colossians 3:23). Listen for the guidance of the Holy Spirit (John 10:27) and for confirmation from trusted believers.

"I married into a family whose women are fine house-keepers, mothers, and cooks. I'm none of these," says Cynthia. "If I begin to worry over a slight, I check in with my husband, who assures me that he loves our life together and how we choose to live it. We also have limited our involvement in Life Groups for professional concerns and soul-care reasons. We have, on occasion, said 'yes.' Dave's job as a counselor prohibits him from having dual relationships with those he counsels. For me, I'm inundated with people and crave solitude to refuel for the next day of teaching."

Myth: When I stumble, it means I'm a failure.

Truth: When you stumble, God will lift you up again. "The LORD upholds all who fall and lifts up all who are bowed down" (Psalm 145:14). Grace increases to meet the need (Romans 5:20–21).

"Praying is how I most feel grace, and allow myself grace," says Sharron. "There is no place safer than with my Father, where I can say without fear, 'I feel like a total failure right now, and I'm desperate for you.' I imagine my head on His lap, and I imagine the words He would say to me. I cry my eyes out and stay there awhile, completely wrung out and open to healing. When I get up I feel stronger and more gracious to myself."

Myth: My imperfections and weaknesses mean God won't be able to use me.

Truth: God is not limited by your ability. His strength shines through your weakness to bring glory to himself (2 Corinthians 12:9).

"The drive for perfection in our current culture has become suffocating to many of us," says Bettina. "We have to embrace a deeper understanding of the concept that we are all broken. When we embrace our imperfections, we allow room for God to work in our life, showing His light through the cracks in our vessel. These imperfections also make us much more approachable as others struggle in their own circumstances. Leaning on God brings us a sense of grace in our struggles which will bless not only us but also those around us."

Myth: I am not enough. My contribution to God is not enough.
Truth: When you bring Him the five loaves and two fish you have, He will bless it abundantly (Matthew 14:16–21). Your offering is enough because *He* is enough.

When Kathy H.'s husband passed away, she knew it would be difficult to care for her parents on her own. "Then a close friend, who had recently been a caregiver to her parents, shared great advice," she told me. "She said, 'Dare to be adequate.' That's a tough lesson for a perfectionist Type A. But I've come to see that just as Jesus multiplied the loaves and the fishes, He will multiply our efforts. He will help us—and our loved ones—get by on 'adequate.'"

Myth: I should be able to do more or better than this.
Truth: God is not glorified by our burnout. Exhaustion does not honor Him. God is glorified when we are satisfied in Him as He leads us "along the right paths for his name's sake" (Psalm 23:3).

Maria admits, "I'm too hard on myself all the time. I often think and say 'I should have done fill-in-the-blank.' I've decided if I quit saying the word *should* I would probably be a much more at-peace person."

I can relate to the struggle with *should*. Last summer I took my kids to a community-wide free lunch program at a local public school, which also offered activities after the lunch. It felt heaven-sent. I didn't have to cook or clean up afterward, and I was able to research for my next novel while the kids played with new friends.

When a TV reporter came to cover the program, both of my kids were interviewed. That night we gathered around the television and watched the six o'clock news. When the reporter asked my daughter why we came, she said, "My mom doesn't want to cook." Well, true enough. No big deal. But two days later at church, a woman came up to me and said, "I saw your kids on the news. Really, how hard is it to feed your own children?"

Ouch. The summer lunch program really felt like God's grace to me, and the kids loved it, too. But that one comment made me question whether I should keep on doing things the hard way, just because I "should be able to." In the end, I opted for more free lunch. I need all the grace I can get. (And all the mamas said, "Amen.")

Myth: I've made too many mistakes; I'm too far gone from God. *Truth*: He longs for your return to Him, and wants to lavish you with grace in the same way the prodigal son's father celebrated him (Luke 15:20–31). "I tell you," Jesus said, "there will be more rejoicing in heaven over one sinner who repents than over ninety-nine righteous persons who do not need to repent" (Luke 15:7).

"To be honest, grace is something I'm learning," admits Kathryn. She shares:

> I feel guilty that I am mad at God, that I don't spend much time with Him, that I have a hard time letting go and going to church. Because of the way I was raised in an extremely legalistic home and church, it's hard for me to accept grace and even understand it. I am coming out of that, thankfully and am learning that God is not just waiting to punish me at any given moment.

Grace for me is realizing that no matter how many mistakes I make, God's still there. It's knowing that I am coming out from my shell of anger and bitterness and God *will* take me back. It's knowing that even if I don't go to church sometimes, God is still with me and loves me even though I feel the guilt. His grace is new every day.

As you look over the seven myths above, is there one you can relate to more than the others? If so, I encourage you to dwell on its accompanying truth. Look up the Scripture reference and commit that verse to memory. The next time one of these myths creeps in to steal grace and replace it with shame, remember that those thoughts are not from God but from the great deceiver. Combat lies with truth!

A STORY OF GRACE IN THE BACKGROUND AND IN THE SPOTLIGHT

By the time she was twelve, Ruth knew what she wanted to do with her life. Raised by her medical missionary parents in China, she would remain single and devote her life to winning souls as a missionary in Tibet.

When she returned to the United States to attend Wheaton College, however, she met a man who would change everything for her. He was "a man of one purpose [that] controls his whole heart and life," she wrote to her parents, "a real inspiration."[2] She was falling in love with him, and he with her.

But there was one problem. Ruth was still convinced her life's purpose was tied to foreign missions. He just as firmly believed that his was not, and he told her to choose between missionary work or a life with him.

That young man was Billy Graham.

Ruth spent months wrestling with God over the question. She and Billy loved each other, but she couldn't deny the unease she felt about giving up her dream. Confiding in her journal, she wrote, "If I marry Bill I must marry him with my eyes open. He will be increasingly burdened for the lost souls and increasingly active in the Lord's work. After the joy and satisfaction of knowing that I am his by rights—and his forever, I will slip into the background. . . . In short, be a lost life. Lost in Bill's."[3]

She struggled even after they became engaged, but after the two wed in 1943, she never spoke with regret of her marriage. "Make the least of all that goes and the most of all that comes," she would say. "And keep looking forward. Don't look backwards."[4]

The press came to call Ruth the "Revival Widow" for how often she was left behind when Billy preached at other churches and his crusades. He was gone more than six months of the year, often for more than a month at a time. In her poetry, she described the good-byes between herself and her husband "like a small death."

Ruth never grew accustomed to the limelight that followed Billy, and by extension, their family. Fans lined up for him at restaurants and airports, strangers stole into their yard to snatch a souvenir stick or rock, and Ruth was scrutinized in the press even as she tried to shield the five children from the spotlight.

Ruth's passion for the lost remained as strong as ever, but when she traveled with Billy during his early crusades, she struggled to understand her purpose. Frustrated during the 1954 London crusade, she journaled, "I don't know where one single contact I have made over here has resulted in one single conversion to Christ."[5]

Over time, it became clear that Ruth excelled in one-on-one ministry, especially to those in prison. She also served a much more vital role in Billy's ministry than most people realized. Ruth and her father were the two people Billy most trusted as advisors and counselors. Having been raised in China and having attended school in Korea, Ruth's burden for the people of Asia remained strong. She encouraged her husband to visit and later accompanied him on his trips to China.[6]

"My father would not have been what he is today if it wasn't for my mother," Ruth's son Franklin said. "She stood strong for what was biblically correct and accurate. She would help my father prepare his messages, listening with an attentive ear, and if she saw something that wasn't right or heard something that she felt wasn't as strong as it could be, she was a voice to strengthen this or eliminate that. Every person needs that kind of input in their life and she was that to my father."[7]

Billy Graham echoed his son's sentiment. "No one else could have borne the load that she carried," he said. "She was a vital and integral part of our ministry, and my work through the years would have been impossible without her encouragement and support."[8]

Ruth Bell Graham thought her purpose—reaching the lost through foreign missions—was swallowed up by Billy's. At least in the early years, she felt her personal contribution to God's kingdom was not enough. But grace perfected God's purpose for her life, even when she didn't understand.

Grace took Ruth's efforts in her husband's life and ministry and multiplied them to reach the lost not just in China but around the world. What she once thought would be a "lost life" was found to be more significant than she imagined.

This is what grace does for all of us. We are enough because God is enough. Our offering is enough because Jesus multiplies it. What we may think is lost is redeemed when we find ourselves in Him.

GRACE: THE PERFECT FIT

Just a few more pages and we'll reach the end of this book together. Whether you read it from cover to cover or just picked the bits and pieces that seemed most relevant to you, I'm so grateful that you've joined me and the women who have boldly lent their stories on this journey. My prayer for you is that you truly do feel free to lean, and that you have peace in your lopsided life. I'm praying that:

- You will courageously live on purpose.
- You'll release any false guilt for focusing your energies, rather than leading a fragmented life.
- You'll step off the broken scales we use to compare ourselves to others.
- You'll choose the best over the good, examining the voices in your head and heart, tuning your ears to the Holy Spirit.
- You'll seize God even when—especially when— you're too exhausted to seize the day.
- You will abide in Christ and nurture consistent connections with others.

- You'll establish boundaries that stretch or tighten when they need to.
- You'll carve out some breathing room, and take care of yourself.
- You'll prayerfully seek God's vision not just for your life but for your day.
- You'll accept the grace that is offered to you, and you will offer it to yourself.

In Matthew 11:28–30, Jesus says, "Come to me, all you who are weary and burdened, and I will give you rest. Take my yoke upon you and learn from me, for I am gentle and humble in heart, and you will find rest for your souls. For my yoke is easy and my burden is light."

At first glance, this doesn't make a whole lot of sense, does it? If we come to Jesus weary and burdened, and He promises rest, why doesn't He lift our load and tell us to run free? Instead, He tells us to yoke ourselves to Him. That means we walk in step with Him. We turn when He turns. We don't run out ahead of Him, but match our pace to His. "This is a different kind of yoke, one perfectly fitted to support and aid us in fulfilling His purpose for our lives," writes Kerri Weems. "When we are yoked to Christ, He carries most of the weight. Being yoked with Him means that we are living in a way that allows us rest because we are under His covering of grace."[9]

Jesus didn't tell His listeners to throw off the yoke completely, because they still had work to do—and so do we. God created work for us to do, both in our big-picture purpose and in our daily calling to represent Him. But when we wear the yoke of grace while shouldering our work, we get to depend on God's strength more than we rely on our human abilities. Most importantly, it keeps us walking close to Jesus wherever our life and work may lead.

I can think of no better way to close this book than with this picture of the yoke of Christ. Are we weary and burdened? God's grace is perfectly fitted to help us fulfill His purpose for our lives. His grace is a perfect fit for each of us. As we lean into the life we've been called to, we won't always get things right. We may say yes or no too often, too soon, or too late. We may neglect or adopt priorities that we shouldn't. We may slip into habits that don't honor God. But listen: when we stumble, God is right there to pull us up again.

Walk in step with Jesus. He will bear most of the weight. Find rest for your soul in His pace for your work. Find rest for your soul in Him.

Everything begins and ends with grace.

Trading Guilt for Grace

As a presidential historian, Jane Hampton Cook frequently appears on CNN and Fox News to provide commentary for current events. But many people don't realize that when she's off camera—and even sometimes when she's on—she suffers with chronic pain.

Debilitating migraines plagued her for years, and despite trying several doctors, tests, and treatments, she's had little relief. The pain has strained her professionally, as an author and news commentator, as well as personally. "As a parent, because of my illnesses I haven't been able to be as active," she says.

For a while Jane felt guilty that her kids weren't enrolled in as many after-school activities, and that she didn't feel well enough to spend more time preparing meals. Instead, she would opt for sandwiches and frozen food. "My mom was a great cook and I often feel guilty that I don't measure up to that standard," she says. "I've had to give myself grace in this area."

Though Jane didn't know why her stamina was limited, she did learn to allow for it. "If I had a speaking event, it would wipe me out for the next couple of days—so I learned to keep my schedule light the day or two after that event so I could rest and recuperate. If I was asked to do TV, then I would try to keep my schedule light in the day or two after the segment."

Over a period of eighteen months, Jane's headaches grew in intensity and became daily, sometimes waking her in the night. After blacking out in the kitchen one afternoon, she continued to have near-blackouts about once a month.

She continued to publish, but her health interfered with her ability to actively promote her latest work, *The Burning of the White House: James and Dolley Madison and the War of 1812.* At home, too, her pain was a daily burden.

"Sometimes I've been so sound-sensitive and light-sensitive from my headaches that I can't handle eating dinner or breakfast with the family because it's just too noisy and too bright," she says.

But the time Jane spent in bed, with the lights off, provided a different opportunity with her three sons. "They've come in and curled up next to me, telling me what's on their minds," she says. "I may not have been able to attend baseball games, but I have hopefully been accessible to their emotional needs and questions and been an encouragement to them in those quiet times."

Finally, a brain MRI revealed the source of Jane's migraines: a condition called Chiari malformation caused the lower part of her cerebellum (called "tonsils") to intrude into her spinal cord, slowing the flow of her spinal fluid. The third neurosurgeon Jane met with told her the shape of the malformation was hitting her brain stem and causing her symptoms.

"I really felt God's grace and presence in that moment because I realized I'd found a surgeon who had truly listened to my symptoms and had closely studied my images," Jane says. "That gave me confidence that God could use this surgeon to bring me healing."

Jane's surgery was successful. And though her recovery time prevented her from commentating during the final month before the contentious 2016 presidential election, she was able to appear on camera again two weeks before the inauguration for several news networks. She also covered the inauguration ceremony and parade live for Fox News Radio.

During that trying period of ill health, without a proper diagnosis, Jane felt at times that she wasn't enough for her family or her job. But, she says, "I've learned to give myself grace by adjusting my expectations of my capabilities and leaning on the help and support of others. I've learned to accept help when people have offered it."

Your Turn

1. Are any of the standards you give yourself unrealistic? If so, how can you adjust those?
2. Are you striving to do something without God's help? If so, why?
3. Which myth about grace have you struggled with?
4. In what area do you need to give yourself more grace?
5. What did you read about grace in this chapter that you most needed to be reminded of?

Truths to Trust

Grace means you don't have to earn God's love.
God's grace is perfectly fitted to help us fulfill His purpose for our lives.

KNOWING JESUS
PERSONALLY

If you have not yet trusted Christ as your Savior, let today be the day that you invite him to be Lord of your life. Without Christ, we have no hope in this life and no hope of enjoying heaven in the next. But because of Christ, we can accept eternal life as a free gift, based on God's grace.

For the wages of sin is death, but the gift of God is eternal life in Christ Jesus our Lord.
ROMANS 6:23

Heaven is not something we can earn or deserve on our own merit. We can't attend enough church services, give enough money to charity, or be good enough in any way to pave our own path to heaven. But the good news is that we don't have to—because God's grace is offered to us as a gift.

For it is by grace you have been saved, through faith—and this is not from yourselves, it is the gift of God—not by works, so that no one can boast.
EPHESIANS 2:8–9

Because we sin, no one deserves to go to heaven. Even the best of us do things that displease God.

For all have sinned and fall short of the glory of God.
ROMANS 3:23

Because God is holy and just, our sin excludes us from His presence.

The wages of sin is death.
ROMANS 6:23

But because God is not willing that anyone should perish, He sent His Son, Jesus Christ, into the world as the perfect, blameless one to die for us. He paid the penalty for our sins and purchased a place in heaven for us.

But God demonstrates his own love for us in this: While we were still sinners, Christ died for us.
ROMANS 5:8

Jesus answered, "I am the way and the truth and the life. No one comes to the Father except through me."
JOHN 14:6

If you believe this much is true, you're on the right track. But you must go one step further and *receive* the gift of salvation by placing your personal faith in Christ—by asking Him to be your Savior and Lord. Faith is turning from your sins and trusting in Jesus Christ alone for your eternal salvation.

Yet to all who did receive him, to those who believed in his name, he gave the right to become children of God.
JOHN 1:12

If you declare with your mouth, "Jesus is Lord," and believe in your heart that God raised him from the dead, you will be saved.
ROMANS 10:9

"Everyone who calls on the name of the Lord will be saved."
ROMANS 10:13

Are you ready to invite Christ into your life? Pray to Him right now, acknowledging your sin and accepting the free gift of eternal life. Ask Him to show you how to live in a way that honors Him. The prayer below may express the desire of your heart:

Dear Lord, thank you for the gift of eternal life. I know I am a sinner and that I cannot save myself. I believe Jesus is the Son of God and that He died for my sins and rose again from the dead. I now put my complete trust in Him alone for eternal life. Thank you for saving me. Now, help me through your Holy Spirit to live a life that honors you. In Jesus's name, amen.

If you have prayed to receive Christ, celebrate! You just made the most important decision that you will ever make in life. Find someone to share your news with, and seek out a Bible-teaching church where you can learn the Word of God and spend time with other Christians. Make Bible reading and prayer a daily priority, and allow God to mold you into the person He wants you to be.

NOTES

If there is no citation for a woman's quote, it's from a personal interview I conducted with her for the exclusive purpose of this book.

Introduction

1. John Ortberg, *The Life You've Always Wanted* (Grand Rapids, MI: Zondervan, 1997), 191.
2. Henry and Richard Blackaby, *God in the Marketplace: 45 Questions Fortune 500 Executives Ask about Faith, Life and Business* (Nashville, TN: B&H Publishing Group, 2010), 170.
3. Bruce B. Miller, *Your Life in Rhythm: Six Rhythm Strategies for a Better Life* (McKinney, TX: Dadlin Press, 2016), 32.

Chapter 1: Life on Purpose

1. Betsey Stevenson and Justin Wolfers, *The Paradox of Declining Female Happiness* (Cambridge, MA: National Bureau of Economic Research, 2009), 28, 40.
2. Viktor E. Frankl, *Man's Search for Meaning* (New York: Pocket Books, 1984), 95.
3. Ibid., 126, 127.
4. Brenda Yoder, *Balance, Busyness, and Not Doing It All: Finding Balance During the Busiest Years of Parenting* (Brenda L. Yoder, 2015), 14.
5. Carolyn Custis James, *When Life and Beliefs Collide* (Grand Rapids, MI: Zondervan, 2001), 72.
6. Susie Larson, *Your Beautiful Purpose: Discovering and Enjoying What God Can Do through You* (Minneapolis, MN: Bethany House Publishers, 2013), 32.
7. Kimberly M. Drew and Jocelyn Green, *Refresh: Spiritual Nourishment for Parents of Children with Special Needs* (Grand Rapids, MI: Kregel, 2016).

Chapter 2: Unapologetically Focused

1. Miller, *Your Life in Rhythm*, 84.
2. Michael McKinney, "Marcus Buckingham and the Truth about You," LeadingBlog, October 6, 2008, http://www.leadershipnow.com/leadingblog/2008/10/marcus _buckingham_and_the_trut.html.
3. Marcus Buckingham, "Know Your Strengths, Own Your Strengths," Lean In (blog), http://leanin.org/education/know-your-strengths-own-your-strengths-no-one -else-will/.
4. "Putting the Strengths-Based Perspective to Work," The Marcus Buckingham Company, 2010, http://tmbc.com/legacy/sites/default/files/services_downloads /Strengths_White_Paper.pdf.
5. Brené Brown, *Daring Greatly: How the Courage to Be Vulnerable Transforms the Way We Live, Love, Parent, and Lead* (New York: Avery Publishing, 2015), 90.

6. Anne Morrow Lindbergh, *Gift from the Sea* (New York: Pantheon, 2005), 40.
7. Miller, *Your Life in Rhythm*, 28.
8. Kerri Weems, *Rhythms of Grace: Discovering God's Tempo for Your Life* (Grand Rapids, MI: Zondervan, 2014), 41–42.
9. Ibid., 41, 35.
10. Ortberg, *The Life You've Always Wanted*, 190.
11. Susie Larson, *Your Sacred Yes: Trading Life-Draining Obligation for Freedom, Passion and Joy* (Minneapolis, MN: Bethany House Publishers, 2015), 164.

Chapter 3: The Myth of Measuring Up

1. Brené Brown, *The Gifts of Imperfection: Let Go of Who You Think You're Supposed to Be and Embrace Who You Are* (Center City, MN: Hazelden, 2010), 94–95.
2. Quote and three studies referenced found in Maria Konnikova, "How Facebook Makes Us Unhappy," *The New Yorker*, September 10, 2013, http://www.newyorker .com/tech/elements/how-facebook-makes-us-unhappy.
3. Jessica Winter, "Selfie-Loathing," *Slate*, July 13, 2013, http://www.slate.com/articles /technology/technology/2013/07/instagram_and_self_esteem_why_the_photo _sharing_network_is_even_more_depressing.html.
4. Rebecca Dube, "'Pinterest stress' afflicts nearly half of moms, survey says," Today.com, May 9, 2013, http://www.today.com/parents/pinterest-stress-afflicts-nearly-half -moms-survey-says-1C9850275.
5. Chip and Joanna Gaines, *The Magnolia Story* (Nashville, TN: Thomas Nelson, 2016), 147.
6. Brown, *The Gifts of Imperfection*, 56.
7. Ibid., 57, 58.
8. Ibid., 65.
9. All quotes in this piece from I Am Second.com, "Shawn Johnson" video, 7:11, posted July 12, 2016. http://www.iamsecond.com/seconds/shawn-johnson/.

Chapter 4: Voices and Choices

1. All quotes by Barry Schwartz from "Barry Schwartz: The Paradox of Choice," Ted Talk transcript, posted September 2006, https://www.ted.com/talks/ barry_schwartz_on_the_paradox_of_choice/transcript?language=en.
2. Madeleine L'Engle, *A Circle of Quiet: The Crosswicks Journal, Book One* (New York: HarperCollins, 1972), 21–22.
3. Priscilla Shirer, *Discerning the Voice of God: How to Recognize When God Speaks* (Chicago, IL: Moody, 2007), 48.
4. Lysa TerKeurst, *The Best Yes: Making Wise Decisions in the Midst of Endless Demands* (Nashville, TN: Thomas Nelson, 2014), 20, 23.
5. Warren Cole Smith, "The Unmaking of Nichole Nordeman," *WORLD*, September 29, 2015, https://world.wng.org/2015/09/the_unmaking_of_nichole_nordeman.
6. Ibid.
7. Mark Moring, "Nichole Nordeman," *Christianity Today*, September 28, 2011, http:// www.christianitytoday.com/ct/2011/septemberweb-only/nordeman-september28 .html?start=1.
8. Smith, "The Unmaking of Nichole Nordeman."

Chapter 5: Seizing God

1. Carolyn Weber, *Holy Is the Day: Living in the Gift of the Present* (Downers Grove, IL: IVP Books, 2013), 97.
2. Laurie Wallin, *Get Your Joy Back: Banishing Resentment and Reclaiming Confidence in Your Special Needs Family* (Grand Rapids, MI: Kregel, 2015), 152.
3. Corrie ten Boom, with Jamie Buckingham, *Tramp for the Lord* (London: Hodder & Stoughton, 1975), 217–218.
4. Weber, *Holy Is the Day*, 99.
5. "Romance of the Youngest Nurse in War of Rebellion," *The* (San Francisco) *Bulletin*, March 9, 1902.
6. Lisa Grunwald and Stephen J. Adler, eds., *Women's Letters: America from the Revolutionary War to the Present* (New York: Dial Press, 2008), 746.

Chapter 6: Consistent Connections

1. "A Rescuer's Journal," by Lt. Iain McConnell, as told to Jocelyn Green. *Today's Christian*, January/February 2006, p. 39.
2. Eric Metaxas, *7 Women and the Secret of Their Greatness* (Nashville, TN: Thomas Nelson, 2015), 41.

Chapter 7: Elastic Boundaries

1. Dr. Henry Cloud and Dr. John Townsend, *Boundaries: When to Say Yes, How to Say No to Take Control of Your Life* (Grand Rapids, MI: Zondervan, 1992), 32–33.
2. Ibid., 28.

Chapter 8: Breathing Room

1. Nancy Gibbs, "How America Has Run Out of Time," *Time*, April 24, 1989, 59.
2. Patti Neighmond, "Overworked Americans Aren't Taking the Vacation They've Earned," Shots: Health News from NPR, July 12, 2016, http://www.npr.org /sections/health-shots/2016/07/12/485606970/ overworked-americans-arent-taking-the-vacation-theyve-earned.
3. Fiona MacRae, "Pace of Life Speeds Up as Study Reveals We're Walking Faster Than Ever," DailyMail.com, May 2, 2007, http://www.dailymail.co.uk/sciencetech /article-452046/Pace-life-speeds-study-reveals-walking-faster-ever.html.
4. Larson, *Your Sacred Yes*, 33.
5. Ibid., 35, 167.
6. Donald Hensrud, M.D., "Is Too Little Sleep a Cause of Weight Gain?", Mayo Clinic website, April 16, 2015, http://www.mayoclinic.org/healthy-lifestyle /adult-health/expert-answers/sleep-and-weight-gain/faq-20058198.
7. Eric J. Olson, M.D., "Lack of Sleep: Can It Make You Sick?", Mayo Clinic Web site, June 9, 2015, http://www.mayoclinic.org/diseases-conditions/insomnia /expert-answers/lack-of-sleep/faq-20057757.
8. "Sleep and Disease Risk," Harvard University Medical School website, December 18, 2007, http://healthysleep.med.harvard.edu/healthy/matters /consequences/sleep-and-disease-risk.
9. Ann Pietrangelo, "The Effects of Sleep Deprivation on the Body," Healthline .com, August 19, 2014, http://www.healthline.com/health/sleep-deprivation /effects-on-body.

10. Julia Steele Rodriguez, "Driving Drowsy vs. Driving Drunk: The Fatal Mistake Most People Make," SleepDr.com, May 2, 2016, https://www.sleepdr.com/the -sleep-blog/driving-drowsy-vs-driving-drunk-the-fatal-mistake-most-people-make/.

11. Brown, *The Gifts of Imperfection,* 106.

12. Warren Wiersbe, "From Fear to Courage," BibleGateway.com, https://www.bible gateway.com/resources/wiersbe-be-bible-study/from-fear-courage-20-19-25.

13. Weems, *Rhythms of Grace*, 49.

Chapter 9: Prayerful Vision

1. Larson, *Your Sacred Yes*, 118.

2. Smith, "The Unmaking of Nichole Nordeman."

3. Phil Vischer, *Me, Myself & Bob: A True Story about Dreams, God and Talking Vegetables* (Nashville, TN: Thomas Nelson, 2006), 236.

4. Ibid., 244.

5. Ibid., 247–248.

6. Ibid., 250.

7. James, *When Life and Beliefs Collide*, 73.

8. The five enemy tactics appeared first in my book *Faith Deployed . . . Again: More Daily Encouragement for Military Wives* (Chicago, IL: Moody Publishers, 2011), 112–113.

9. Chip and Joanna Gaines with Mark Dagostino, *The Magnolia Story* (Nashville, TN: Thomas Nelson, 2016), 123.

10. Ibid., 82.

11. Ibid., 129.

12. Ibid., 130.

13. Ibid., 144.

14. Ibid., 178.

15. Ibid., 181–182.

Chapter 10: Amazing Grace

1. Weems, *Rhythms of Grace*, 189.

2. Ibid., 61

3. Ruth Bell Graham, quoted in Patricia Cornwell, *Ruth, A Portrait: The Story of Ruth Bell Graham* (New York: Doubleday, 1997), 75.

4. Ibid., 76.

5. Michelle DeRusha, *50 Women Every Christian Should Know* (Grand Rapids, MI: Baker Books, 2014), 342.

6. Ruth Bell Graham, quoted in Cornwell, *Ruth: A Portrait*, 169.

7. Ted Olsen, "Ruth Graham Bell Dies at 87," ChristianityToday.com, June 14, 2007, http://www.christianitytoday.com/gleanings/2007/june/ruth-bell-graham-dies-at -87.html

8. Ibid.

9. Ibid.

10. Weems, *Rhythms of Grace*, 61.

ACKNOWLEDGMENTS

With every book I write, I have a host of people to thank—but for this one I have more than ever. I owe a debt of gratitude to nearly fifty women who took time to tell me their stories for the purpose of sharing them through these pages. Your insights make this book far richer than I could have made it on my own.

Thanks also to:

- Andrew Rogers at Discovery House for asking if I had any books on my heart, and to the Breathe Christian Writers Conference for creating a way for me to meet Andy.
- Miranda Gardner, Paul Muckley, and the rest of the editorial team at Discovery House, along with the marketing team, for their excellence as they have leaned into this project with me.
- My agent, Tim Beals of Credo Communications, for not letting me give up on this project right before it received a contract.
- Those who faithfully prayed me through this deadline whenever I cried out for help.
- My parents, Peter and Pixie Falck, for support with the kids and for bringing us food while I wrote. Thanks also to my sister-in-law Audrey Falck for making meals for my family!

Special thanks to my husband, Rob, who took vacation time to help me meet this deadline, even when he was swamped with his own priorities. You always bring perspective and humor to my days. You are God's grace to me.

Finally, thank you, Lord, for writing this book on my heart over the last several years, and for being the Author of my life's story. Help me ever and always to lean into you.

ABOUT THE AUTHOR

Jocelyn Green inspires faith and courage in her readers as an award-winning author of both fiction and nonfiction. A graduate of Taylor University, she loves Mexican food, Broadway musicals, Toblerone chocolate bars, the color red, and reading on her patio. She lives with her husband, Rob, and two children in Cedar Falls, Iowa. *Free to Lean* is her fourteenth book. Visit her at jocelyngreen.com.

Enjoy this book? Help us get the word out!

Share a link to the book or
mention it on social media

Write a review on your blog, on a retailer site,
or on our website (dhp.org)

Pick up another copy to share with someone

Recommend this book for your
church, book club, or small group

Follow Discovery House on
social media and join the discussion

Contact us to share your thoughts:

 @discoveryhouse    @DiscoveryHouse

Discovery House
P.O. Box 3566
Grand Rapids, MI 49501 USA

Phone: 1-800-653-8333
Email: books@dhp.org
Web: dhp.org